The Pattern Library

CROCHET
MEDALLIONS

The Pattern Library
CROCHET MEDALLIONS

Editor
Melanie Miller

BALLANTINE BOOKS · NEW YORK

First published in Great Britain in 1984 by
Ebury Press, National Magazine House,
72 Broadwick Street, London W1V 2BP

The Pattern Library CROCHET MEDALLIONS was conceived,
edited and designed by Dorling Kindersley Limited,
9 Henrietta Street, London WC2

Library of Congress Catalog Card Number: 84–90816

ISBN 0–345–31875–7

Manufactured in the United States of America

First Ballantine Books Edition: October 1984
10 9 8 7 6 5 4 3 2 1

Contents

❖

❖

Introduction

Crochet is one of the most versatile and satisfying handicrafts. All that is needed to produce beautiful, creative and original articles is a hook and some yarn. It appeals to both the novice and the expert alike as the basic techniques are easy to master, and all stitches are variations on a few basics. Yet the permutations are endless, so experienced handicrafters can try all manner of elaborate combinations.

As with other textiles, the origins of crochet are difficult to trace. The technique of crochet appears to have travelled extensively, early samples of it have been found in all corners of the globe — in the Far East, Near East, Africa, Europe, South and North America. These early examples fall into two distinctly different categories: either the crochet has been worked on fine hooks with fine yarns, thus producing a delicate open, lacy fabric, or it has been worked with thicker yarn on large hooks to form a dense fabric. The denser type of crochet was used by the Chinese to make three-dimensional sculptural dolls; the Africans used it for making caps for their chieftains; the Turks used it for making hats, and in Scotland it was used for caps and heavy cloaks.

The more delicate, lace-like form of crochet originated in Italy in the sixteenth century where it was worked by nuns to make church trimmings and vestments, hence the name for it at that time of nun's lace. It was made from very fine cotton yarn on the finest crochet hooks. The technique spread to Spain and to Ireland where it was also worked by nuns for the church.

Nowadays the two different kinds of crochet overlap. Many different types of yarn can be used to give different effects — fine cotton and silks will produce a delicate, cobwebby fabric, reminiscent of Victorian handiwork, bulky yarn can be used for warm, hardwearing garments and household articles. Crochet is not limited to ordinary wool and cotton yarn — any thin, pliable medium may be used. For interesting textures raffia, string or ribbons can be used on their own or mixed with other, more conventional yarns. Experiment with different yarns in the same shade for interesting and unusual results — try combining mohair and slub cotton, or lurex and string.

When making articles from several pieces of crochet, the scope for imaginative design is limitless. A riot of different colors can be used in one article at random, using up scraps of leftover yarn, or a carefully planned design may be worked out, perhaps using subtle shades and texture changes. Simple designs may be as effective as more complex, elaborately planned patterns. One of the beauties of crochet is its versatility — thick yarn and a big hook can quickly produce a bright, bold cushion, or hours of work can go into creating an heirloom bedspread or tablecloth using one of the lace patterns.

BASIC TECHNIQUES

HOOKS

Crochet hooks are usually made from plastic, aluminum or steel. Steel hooks are very fine, and are used mainly for working with fine cotton. Aluminum and plastic hooks range in size from fine to very coarse, and may be used with varying weights of yarn. Since the hooks do not hold stitches but hold only the working loop, they are all made to a standard length.

WHICH YARN?

Choose the most appropriate yarn, hook and stitch pattern to suit your special needs. Generally, very fine yarns and hooks are used for delicate lacy effects, medium-weights for more practical fabrics, heavy-weights for warmth and hard-wearing qualities. If you are making something which needs frequent laundering, choose a machine-washable yarn.

YARNS

In addition to a very wide range of specially-produced crochet threads, most yarns that are manufactured for knitting, knotting and weaving can be used.

Yarn describes any thread spun from natural fibers such as wool, cotton, linen, silk, or synthetics. **Ply** indicates the number of spun single threads which have been twisted together to produce a specific yarn. Single threads may be spun to any thickness so that ply does not refer to a standard thickness of yarn, although the terms 2-, 3- and 4-ply are often used to describe yarns of a recognised thickness. In this book the term "medium-weight" is used instead of "4-ply".

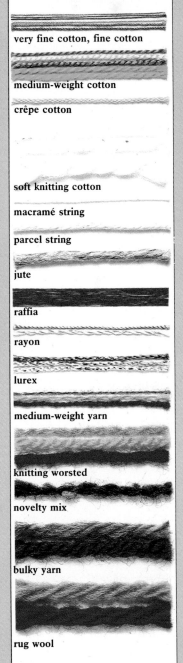

very fine cotton, fine cotton

medium-weight cotton

crêpe cotton

soft knitting cotton

macramé string

parcel string

jute

raffia

rayon

lurex

medium-weight yarn

knitting worsted

novelty mix

bulky yarn

rug wool

HOLDING THE HOOK AND YARN

Shown below are two different ways of holding the hook and yarn, however these methods are not definitive. The right way is the way you find comfortable and easy, and which results in crochet that is regular and even.

THREADING YARN

Threading the yarn through the fingers is important as this helps to give extra tension, controlling the yarn while allowing it to flow easily from hand to hook. If you are left-handed the method is the same.

Threading yarn around the little finger

Pass the working end of yarn around the little finger, over the next finger, under the middle finger and finish with it resting over the forefinger.

Threading yarn over the little finger

Pass the working end of yarn over the little finger, under the next 2 fingers and finish with it resting over the forefinger.

HOLDING THE HOOK

The crochet hook can be held in either the knife or the pencil position. Both ways are equally good and the choice depends on which position feels most comfortable in the hand.

The pencil position

1 *Hold the hook in the right hand like a pencil. If you are left-handed hold the hook in the same way, but in the left hand.*

2 *Prepare to make the first chain by drawing the yarn from the left forefinger with the hook through the slip loop.*

The knife position

1 *Hold the hook in the right hand like a knife. If you are left-handed hold the hook in the same way, but in the left hand.*

2 *Prepare to make the first chain by drawing the yarn from the left forefinger with the hook through the slip loop.*

THE FOUNDATION CHAIN

To begin crochet, a slip loop is placed on the hook. This is a working loop and is never counted as a stitch. Stitches are made by pulling one loop through another to form a foundation chain upon which the next row or round is worked.

CHAIN STITCH (ch)

1 *Hold back with slip loop in RH, twist hook under and over yarn.*

2 *Draw yarn through slip loop on hook.*

A length of chain sts.

DOUBLE CHAIN STITCH (dch)

1 *Make slip loop and work 2 ch, insert hook into 1st ch, yarn over hook (yo), draw loop through.*

2 *Yarn over hook, draw through both loops on hook. Repeat steps 1 and 2.*

Use dchs for firm edge.

FINISHING OFF

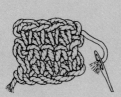

COUNTING

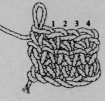

1 *Complete final st and cut yarn about 6in from work. Pull through last loop and tighten.*

2 *Thread loose end into yarn needle and darn into back of work.*

Count sc as above. In doubles count 1 upright as 1 st. Count 1 ch between 2 dc as 3 sts.

TURNING CHAINS (t-ch)

Extra chains are worked at the end of a row before turning to bring the hook to the correct depth of the stitch being worked, so that the first stitch can be made evenly.

Table giving number of turning chains required for each stitch

single crochet: 1 turning chain
half double: 2 turning chains
double: 3 turning chains
treble: 4 turning chains
double treble: 5 turning chains

BASIC STITCHES

Each stitch gives a different texture and varies in depth, and every row makes a new chain line into which the next row is worked. Where stitches are worked back and forth in rows there is no right or wrong side to the work. *NB:* turning chain (**t-ch**) forms first stitch in row.

SLIP STITCH (ss)

1 *Make no. of ch. Insert hook from F to B into 2nd ch from hook.*

2 *Yo, draw through 2 loops on hook. Repeat steps 1 and 2 to end.*

3 *Make 1 t-ch, turn, insert hook into B of first st of last row.*

SINGLE CROCHET (sc)

  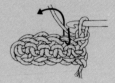

1 *Make ch row. Insert hook into 2nd ch from hook, yo, draw through.*

2 *Yo, draw through 2 loops. Repeat steps 1 and 2 to end.*

3 *1 t-ch, turn, insert hook under both loops of 1st st of last row.*

HALF DOUBLE (hdc)

1 *Make ch row. Yo and insert into 3rd ch, yo, draw through.*

2 *Yo, draw through 3 loops. Cont working hdc into every ch to end.*

3 *2 t-chs, turn. Make 1 hdc into 1st st of last row, rep to end.*

DOUBLE CROCHET (dc)

  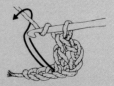

1 *Make ch row. Yo, insert into 5th ch, yo, draw 1 loop through.*

2 *Yo, draw through first 2 lps on hook, rep once more.*

3 *Cont to end, 3 t-ch, turn. Make 1 dc into 2nd st of last row.*

TREBLE (tr)

1 *Make ch row. Yo twice, insert into 6th ch from hook, yo, draw lp through.*

2 *Yo and draw through first 2 lps on hook. Rep step 2 twice more.*

3 *Cont to end, make 4 t-ch, turn. Make first tr into 2nd st of row below.*

DOUBLE TREBLE (dtr)

1 *Make ch row. Yo 3 times, insert into 7th ch from hook, yo, draw loop through.*

2 *Yo and draw through first 2 lps on hook. Rep this step 3 times more.*

3 *Cont to end, make 5 t-ch, turn. Make first dtr into 2nd st of row below.*

OPENWORK STITCHES

Openwork mesh patterns are formed by missing stitches and working chains over the spaces left; the simplest way to make lacy crochet. Various patterns can be made by altering the combination of stitches and spaces.

Simple openwork
Work 1 dc, 2ch, miss 2 ch in pre-vious row, 1 dc into next ch. Rep to end.

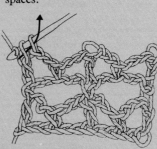

Bar and lattice
1 dc, 3 ch, miss 2 ch in row below, 1 sc into next ch, 3 ch, miss 2 ch. Rep to end.

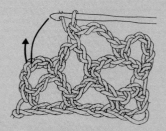

Simple net ground
Work 1 sc into 5th ch of row below, 5 ch, rep to end.

BASIC STITCH VARIATIONS

Interesting variations to the basic stitches are made by inserting the hook into different parts of the stitch below and twisting the yarn in different ways.

Crossed single crochet
Work as for sc but take hook over yarn and draw loop through.

Working into half of stitch below
For RS ridge, insert hook into back of st in row below; into front of st for WS ridge.

Working between stitches
Insert hook into space between 2 sts in row below.

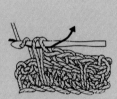

Working into stitches 2 rows below
Insert hook front to back between 2 sts, 2 rows below.

Working into chain space
Insert hook into space between ch sts in row below.

Working a raised effect
Insert hook from front around st below. For indented effect, insert hook from back.

TEXTURED STITCHES

Textures are created by working into the same stitch several times, as in bobble patterns, or by wrapping the yarn around the hook several times before drawing through, as in bullion stitch.

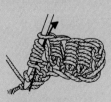

Bobble stitch
5 dc into next st, withdraw hook, insert into 1st dc, pick up lp, draw through.

Bullion stitch
Yo several times, insert hook into ch, yo, draw through, yo, draw through all loops.

Cabling around stitch
Yo, insert hook from back to front around dc in row below, work 1 dc.

WORKING IN THE ROUND

Working in the round instead of in rows means that the foundation row of chains is made into a circle or ring and the crochet stitches are then worked from this circle in a continuous round without turning and working back and forth. Many different shapes can be made from this simple foundation ring: round medallions are made by increasing evenly around the circle; square medallions are made by increasing at four regular intervals; hexagons are made by increasing at six regular intervals, and octagons are made by increasing at eight regular intervals. The medallions can be plain, lace or relief, in one solid color or a mixture of shades. Medallions usually start with a foundation ring of chains.

Single chain ring

Make a foundation chain to required length and then close ring with a slip stitch into the first chain.

Single crochet ring

If a large number of chains is needed for a medallion, work the ring in single crochet.

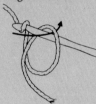 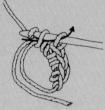 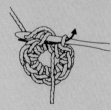

1 *Make a circle with yarn as shown. Insert hook, yo, draw through circle, yo, draw through loop.*

2 *Work required number of sc around circle and over both strands.*

3 *Pull loose end firmly to draw circle together. Close ring with a slip stitch.*

Beginning a round

In many of the patterns, the first instruction in round 1 is to chain 1, 2, 3 or more. These chains bring the hook up to the height of the stitches which will then be made into the ring. Although they do not resemble a stitch, these chains are the equivalent of the first stitch of the round. For example:

Round 1 3ch, 1ldc into ring.

To allow room for subsequent stitches to fit into the ring, slide the stitches along the ring.

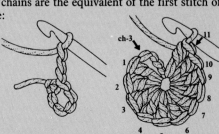

Ending a round

When all the stitches of a round have been made, the first and last stitches are joined with a slip stitch.

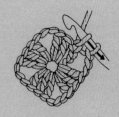

Insert the hook into the third (top) chain of the initial ch-3, pull through a loop, pull the new loop through the loop on the hook, thereby making a slip stitch.

COLORWORK MEDALLIONS

Colorwork medallions are composed of two or more colors. As well as being decorative, they are an economic way of using up odd scraps of yarn. In colorwork medallions, new colors are added at the beginning of rounds. When breaking off the old yarn at the end of a round and joining in the new color, secure the ends carefully.

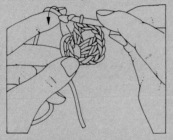

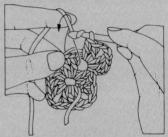

Securing loose end on first round
On first round of medallion, work stitches over loose end.

Securing loose ends on subsequent rounds
When joining in new colors on subsequent rounds work several stitches over loose ends of new and old yarn. When medallion is completed trim ends.

Joining in new colors

There are several different ways of joining in new yarn, two of which are shown below. The exact place where new yarn should be joined is indicated in the pattern instructions.

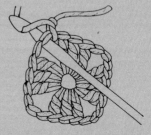

1 *Insert end of new yarn through space where second round is to begin. Make a knot by tying the two ends together.*

2 *Tighten knot, leaving an end of yarn about 3in long, and have knot fall at far right corner of space. Insert hook into space and pull through a loop. Continue working next round.*

Make a slip knot in the new yarn, leaving an end of yarn about 3in long. Insert hook into loop then insert hook into space indicated in medallion instructions, pull through another loop. Work a slip stitch, pulling new loop through original loop on hook. Continue working next round.

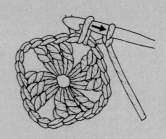

BLOCKING

Depending on the type of yarn used, crochet medallions may need to be blocked. Individual pieces may be blocked before being sewn together, or a completed project may be blocked after it has been joined.

Place the crochet right side down on a padded surface or ironing board. Pin evenly around the edges. Using a damp cloth and a warm iron, (or as instructed on the ball band), press lightly and evenly, lifting the iron up and down, not to and fro. Do not let the full weight of the iron rest on the crochet. Leave the crochet to cool, and then remove the pins.

Blocking lace and relief crochet

Depending on the intended use of the article, lace designs may be starched before being blocked. Relief crochet should be placed face down over a thick, heavy towel, so that the raised texture of the work is not flattened.

Joining completed medallions together

Depending on the finish required, there are several different ways of joining medallions together.

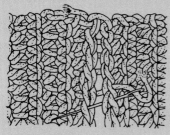

Woven seam
For a very neat, almost invisible seam, lay the medallions wrong side up with edges touching. Thread a needle with matching yarn and weave it loosely around centers of the edge stitches of both pieces.

Sewn seam
Place one medallion on top of another, with right sides together. Thread a needle with matching yarn and oversew the edge stitches of both medallions together.

Single crochet seam
Place one medallion on top of another, with right sides together. Insert the hook from front to back through the edges of both medallions, yo and draw through, work 1sc in the usual way and then insert the hook into the next stitch along ready to make the next sc.

Slip-stitched seam

Place one medallion on top of another, with right sides together. Insert the hook from front to back through the edge stitches of both pieces, yo and draw through. Work one ss in the usual way, then insert the hook into the next stitch along, ready to make the next ss.

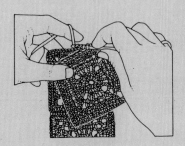

Joining as you go

When making squares, hexagons or octagons, sometimes the second medallion may be joined to the first while working the last round of the second. Specific instructions are given with the patterns. Subsequent medallions may be joined on one or more sides.

Fillers

After circles or octagons have been joined together, quite large spaces may be left between them. These spaces can be filled with small filler designs. Instructions for these are given with some patterns, or one of the small motifs from the fillers and motifs section may be used.

BORDERS
Single crochet border

After all the medallions have been joined together, the edge can be finished off with one or more rounds of single crochet.

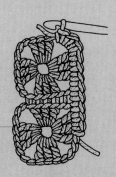

Attach a matching or contrasting yarn to the edge of the piece. Insert the hook from front to back through the edge. Yo and draw through. Work a single crochet and then continue evenly along the edge, working a sc in every stitch or in every other stitch. In the corner stitch or space, work three sc. At the end of the round, join with a ss into the first sc.

Fringed border

Before adding a fringe there must be a border of one or two rows of single crochet.

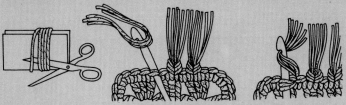

1 *Wind yarn around a carboard gauge which is the desired depth of the completed fringe. Cut ends at one side.*

2 *Fold 3 or 4 strands in half, insert hook in stitch and pull the loop of the strands through the stitch.*

3 *Pull the strands through the loop, and then, to tighten the knot, pull the strands away from the edge.*

CALCULATING THE NUMBER OF MEDALLIONS REQUIRED

Use this method for working out the number of squares, circles, octagons or hexagons required.

1. Decide the length and width you'd like the finished article to be.
2. Crochet one medallion in the yarn you intend to use, then measure the width of the finished medallion.

3. Divide the length of the afghan, cushion, or whatever it is you are going to make by the width of the medallion, then divide the width of your proposed article by the width of the medallion.

4. Multiply these two figures together, and the resulting figure is the number of medallions you require.

Example

To make an afghan measuring 72in long by 54in wide, using a medallion 6in wide:

$72 \div 6 = 12$
$54 \div 6 = 9$
$12 \times 9 = 108$

So total number of medallions required is 108.

SUGGESTED SIZES

Afghans
Suggested approximate sizes:
45in × 60in, 54in × 72in, 60in × 80in.

Tablecloths
Take the measurements from an existing tablecloth, or drape a sheet over the table and take the appropriate measurements from that.

Bedspreads
Take the measurements from an existing bedspread, or drape a sheet over the bed and take the appropriate measurements from that.

Cushions
Can be round or square, any size from 10in to 20in across.

Place mats
Round or square, 8in to 12in across; rectangular, 8in to 12in wide by 12in to 18in long.

SUGGESTED PATTERNS

Crochet medallions may be joined together in an infinite number of ways to produce afghans, bedspreads, cushions, tablecloths, place mats, coasters, rugs, shawls, bags, or other household or personal objects. The medallions may be joined together at random, or a uniform pattern may be designed. Some suggestions for the layout of medallions are shown overleaf.

SQUARES AND OCTAGONS

HEXAGONS AND CIRCLES

SIZE GUIDE

Each pattern includes information as to the size of the hook and the type of yarn used to produce the particular medallion illustrated. By using thicker or thinner yarn, or a larger or smaller hook, the size of the medallion can be varied.

HOOK AND YARN GUIDE

14	very fine cotton	F	knitting worsted, mohair
12		G	
10		H	
7		I	
		J	
7	fine cotton and	J	Aran-type, thick knitting worsted
4	equivalent yarn	K	
0		L	
B			
C			
C	medium-weight yarn	L	bulky, heavy-weight yarn
D		M	
E		N	
F			

ABBREVIATIONS

alt	alternate(ly)	pc	picot
B	back	RDB	round double back
beg	beginning	RDF	round double front
ch(s)	chain(s)	rem	remain(ing)
cl	cluster	rep	repeat
cont	continu(e)(ing)	rnd	round
dec	decreas(e)(ing)	RS	right side
dc	double crochet	sc	single crochet
dch(s)	double chain(s)	ss	slip stitch
dtr	double treble	sp(s)	space(s)
F	front	st(s)	stitch(es)
gr(s)	group(s)	tog	together
hdc	half double	tr	treble
inc	increas(e)(ing)	t-ch(s)	turning chain(s)
lp(s)	loop(s)	WS	wrong side
no.	number	yo	yarn over hook

A star * shown in a pattern row denotes that the stitches shown after this sign must be repeated from that point.

Round brackets ( ), enclosing a particular stitch combination, denote that the stitch combination must be repeated in the order shown.

Round brackets at the end of a round, enclosing a number of stitches, denote the total number of stitches worked in that round.

Hyphens refer to those stitches which have already been made but which will be used as the base for the next stitch, eg., you would work 2tr into 2-ch sp, by making 2 trebles into the space created by the chain stitches worked in the previous row.

SQUARES

Squares are the most versatile of the basic shapes. It is easy to join them together and they can be made into a vast range of articles, from cushion covers, bags and scarves, to bedspreads and tablecloths. One of the most traditional crochet patterns is the granny, or Afghan square, p.44. This design can be made into a striking blanket when individual squares are worked with carefully graded bright colors at the center, and edged and joined in one dark color, to give the effect of stained glass windows.

Tudor rose

Size Crochet hook size E and medium-weight yarn produce a square 2½in across.
Materials and uses Use fine, soft, machine-washable yarn for a baby's blanket, or multi-colored bulky yarn for an afghan.

Using A, make 6ch and join into a ring with a ss into first ch.
Round 1 2ch,1dc into ring,(1ch, 4dc in ring) 3 times, 1ch, 2dc into ring.
Round 2 Ss to first 1ch space, (2ch, 2dc, 2ch, 3dc) in same space, (3dc, 2ch, 3dc) in each of next 3 1ch spaces, ss in top of 2ch. Break off A.

Round 3 Joining B to first 2ch space, (3ch, 3tr, 3ch, 4tr) in first 2ch space, (4tr, 3ch, 4tr) in each of next 3 2ch spaces, ss in top of 2ch. Break off B.
Round 4 Join in C to ss, 1sc in each st and 4sc in each 3ch space to end of round, ss in first sc. Fasten off.

Rainbow

Size Crochet hook size F and knitting worsted produce a square 4¼in across.

Materials and Uses Use leftover brightly colored bulky wool for cheerful cushion covers, or make a bedspread from novelty bouclé or tweedy yarn.

This square uses 6 colors, A, B, C, D, E and F.

Using A, make 4ch, and join into a ring with a ss into first ch.

Round 1 4ch, 3tr into ring, (2ch, 4tr into ring) 3 times, 2ch, join with a ss to 4th of first 4ch. Break off A and turn.

Round 2 (RS) Join in B to any 2ch space, 2sc into same space, (1sc into each of next 4sts, 2sc, 2ch, 2sc into corner 2ch space) 3 times, 1sc into each of next 4sts, 2sc into same space as join, 2ch, join with a ss to first sc. Break off B and turn.

Round 3 Join in C to first sc after a 2ch space, 3ch, 1dc into 2ch space before join, *(miss next sc, 1dc into next sc, 1dc into missed sc) 3 times, miss 1sc, 1dc into next 2ch space, 1dc into missed sc, 1dc into next sc, 1dc into 2ch space before last dc; repeat from * 3 times omitting last 2dc at end of last repeat; join with a ss to 3rd of first 3ch. Break off C and turn.

Round 4 Join in D to same place as ss of last round, 3ch, 2dc into same space, (1ch, 3dc into next dc, 1dc into each of next 8dc, 3dc into next dc) 4 times omitting 3dc at end of last repeat, join with a ss to 3rd of first 3ch. Break off D and turn.

Round 5 Join in E to first dc after any 1ch space, 1sc into same place as join, 1sc into next dc, *(1tr into next dc, then bending tr in half to form bobble on RS of square work 1sc into next dc, 1sc into next dc) 4 times, 3dc into corner 1ch space, 1sc into each of next 2dc; repeat from * 3 times omitting 2sc at end of last repeat, join with a ss to first sc. Break off E and turn.

Round 6 Join in F to first sc of any side, (1sc into each st to center dc of 3dc at corner, 3sc into corner dc) 4 times, 1sc in next dc, join with a ss to first sc. Fasten off.

Daisy square

Size Crochet hook size F and knitting worsted produce a square 2¾in across.

Materials and uses Make place mats from brightly colored cotton crêpe, or use scraps of knitting worsted or bulky yarn for a baby's blanket.

This square uses 3 colors, A, B and C.

Using A, make 4ch and join into a ring with a ss into first ch.

Round 1 1ch, 8sc into ring, join with a ss to first ch. Break off A.

Round 2 Join in B to any sc, ss into same place as join, (4ch, leaving last loop of each tr on hook work 2tr into same place as last ss, yo and draw through all three loops, 4ch, ss into same place as last ss − petal worked −, ss into next sc) 8 times, working ss at end of last repeat in same sc as join. Break off B.

Round 3 Join in C to top of any petal, (1sc into top of petal, 3ch, 1sc into top of next petal, 5ch) 4 times, join with a ss to first sc.

Round 4 1sc into same place as ss, (1sc into each of next 3ch, 1sc into next sc, 1sc into each of next 2ch, 3sc into next ch − corner worked − 1sc into each of next 2ch, 1sc into next sc) 4 times, omitting 1sc at end of last repeat, join with a ss to first sc. Fasten off.

Bermuda triangle

Size Crochet hook size D and medium-weight wool produce a square 3¾in across (row 4 repeated once).

Materials and uses Use pretty pastel colors and soft yarn for a baby's shawl or blanket, or join nine or more for cushion covers.

This design uses 5 colors, A, B, C, D and E.

Row 1 Using A, 4ch, 2dc in 4th ch from hook, 5ch, turn.

Row 2 2dc in 4th ch from hook, 1ch, 3dc in 3rd ch of 3-ch, 5ch, turn.

Row 3 2dc in 4th ch from hook, 1ch, 3dc in 1-ch space, 1ch, 3dc in 3rd ch of 3-ch, 5ch, turn.

Row 4 2dc in 4th ch from hook, (1ch, 3dc) in each 1-ch space across, 1ch, 3dc in 3rd ch of 3-ch, 5ch, turn. Repeat row 4 as many times as you wish. Make 3 more motifs, with B, C and D, each having the same number of rows. Sew them together to form a square. Using E, work single crochet edging all around.

Star bright

Size Crochet hook size E and medium-weight wool produce a square 2½in across.

Materials and uses Make a bright, warm bedspread from leftover bulky yarn, or use knitting worsted for an afghan.

This design uses 2 colors, A and B. Using A, make 6ch and join into a ring with a ss into first ch.

Round 1 1ch, *sc in ring, 3ch, tr in ring, 3ch, tr in ring, 3ch; repeat from * 3 more times, ending with ss in first sc made (4 petals). Break off A.

Round 2 Join in B to a tr following the 3-ch at center of a petal, 1ch, sc in same tr, *sc in top st of next 3-ch, 2dc in sc between petals, sc in top st of next 3-ch, sc in next tr, sc in next ch, 3ch, miss 1ch, sc in next ch, sc in next tr; repeat from * around, ending with 3ch, sc in ch preceding first sc made, join with a ss to first sc.

Round 3 3ch (to count as dc), dc in each st to corner 3-ch, in corner 3-ch make dc, 3ch and dc. Continue thus around, join with a ss to 3rd st of 3-ch first made. Fasten off.

Lazy daisy

Size Crochet hook size F and knitting worsted produce a square 3¼in across.
Materials and uses Use silky yarn for a shawl, or acrylic yarn for a luncheon set.

This square uses 2 colors, A and B. Using A, make 10ch and join into a ring with a ss into first ch.
Round 1 (10ch, sc into ring) 12 times. Break off A.
Round 2 Join in B to any 10-ch loop, 3ch, (2dc, 2ch, 3dc) in same loop, *3hdc in each of next 2 loops, (3dc, 2ch, 3dc) in next loop; repeat from * twice more, work 3hdc in each of last 2 loops, join with a ss to 3rd ch of 3-ch. Fasten off.

Crossed square

Size Crochet hook size E and medium-weight cotton produce a square 4¼in across.
Materials and uses Use slub linen for a bedspread, or use thick chenille for pot holders.

This square uses 2 colors, A and B.
Note *Cluster (cl): work 3dc keeping last loop of each st on hook, draw a loop through all sts on hook.*
Using A, make 8ch and join into a ring with a ss into first ch.
Round 1 2ch, into ring work (1cl, 2ch, 1cl, 5ch) 4 times, join with a ss.
Round 2 2ch, *3dc into 2ch loop (2ch, 1cl, 3ch, 1cl, 2ch) into 5ch loop; rep from * 3 more times, join with a ss to 2nd of 2ch. Break off A.
Round 3 Join in B to joining ss with a ss and 2ch, *1dc into each dc, 2dc into 2ch loop (2ch, 1cl, 3ch, 1cl, 2ch) into 3ch loop, 2dc into 2ch loop; rep from * 3 more times, join with a ss.
Round 4 2ch, work as round 3 from * 4 times, ending 1dc into each of last 2dc, join with a ss to 2nd of 2ch.
Round 5 As round 4, ending 1dc into each of last 4dc, join with a ss to 2nd of 2ch. Fasten off.

Arched square

Size Crochet hook size D and medium-weight cotton produce a square 3½in across.

Materials and uses Use fine cotton for tablecloth insertion and border, or join nine or more made from medium-weight yarn or knitting worsted for a cushion cover.

Make 8ch and join into a ring with a ss into first ch.

Round 1 3ch, 2dc into ring, 7ch, (3dc, 7ch) 7 times into ring, join with a ss to top of 3ch.

Round 2 Ss into next 7ch loop, 3ch, 2dc into same loop, 2ch, 3dc into same loop, *7ch, miss next loop, (3dc, 2ch, 3dc) into next loop; repeat from * twice more, 7ch, miss last loop, join with a ss to top of first 3ch.

Round 3 3ch, 1dc into each of next 2dc, *(2dc, 2ch, 2dc) into corner space, 1dc into each of next 3dc, 7ch, 1dc into each of next 3dc; repeat from * twice more, (2dc, 2ch, 2dc) into corner space, 1dc into each of next 3dc, 7ch, join with a ss to top of first 3ch.

Round 4 3ch, 1dc into each of next 4dc, *(2dc, 2ch, 2dc) into corner space, 1dc into each of next 5dc, 4ch, 1sc into missed 7ch loop of round 1 and enclosing chains of 2nd and 3rd rounds, 4ch, 1dc into each of next 5dc; repeat from * 3 more times, omitting last 5dc, join with a ss to top of first 3ch. Fasten off.

Bull's-eye

Size Crochet hook size F and knitting worsted produce a square 4½in across.

Materials and uses Make a warm afghan from scraps of bulky or knitting worsted, or use thick acrylic yarn for a quick-drying mat for the bathroom.

This square uses 4 colors, A, B, C and D.

Using A, make 4ch and join into a ring with a ss into first ch.

Round 1 3ch, 11dc into ring (12dc), join with a ss to 3rd ch of 3-ch. Break off A.

Round 2 Join in B to any dc, 3ch, dc in same st, work 2dc in each dc around (24dc), join with a ss to 3rd ch of 3-ch. Break off B.

Round 3 Join in C to any dc, 3ch, dc in same st, *dc in next dc, 2dc in next dc; repeat from * around (36dc), join with a ss to 3rd ch of 3-ch. Break off C.

Round 4 Join in D to any dc st, 4ch, 4tr in same st, *in next 8 sts work dc, 6hdc, dc, 5tr in next st; repeat from * around, join with a ss to 4th ch of 4-ch.

Round 5 3ch, dc in next dc and every dc till corner tr st (center tr of 5-tr group), *5dc into corner tr st, dc in every st till next corner tr; repeat from * around, join with a ss to 3rd ch of 3-ch. Fasten off.

Cart-wheel

Size Crochet hook size F and medium-weight wool produce a square 3¾in across.

Materials and uses Use leftover yarn to make a blanket or cushion covers.

This square uses 3 colors, A, B, and C.

Using A, make 5ch and join into a ring with a ss into first ch.

Round 1 5ch, (tr in ring, 1ch) 11 times, join with a ss to 4th ch of 5-ch. Break off A.

Round 2 Join in B to any 1-ch space, pull up loop on hook to ¾in, make puff st in same space – (yo, pull up loop in space to ¾in) 3 times, yo and through all 7 loops on hook, 1ch, make another puff st in same place, *(puff st, 1ch, puff st, 1ch) in next space; repeat from * 10 times, join with a ss to top of first puff st. Break off B (24 puff sts around).

Round 3 Join in C to any 1-ch space, 6ch, tr in same space, *1ch, dc in next space, (1ch, hdc in next space) 3 times, 1ch, dc in next space, 1ch, (tr, 2ch, tr) in next space; repeat from * around, working 2 more corners, after last dc, 1ch, join with a ss to 4th ch of 6-ch.

Round 4 Ss into corner 2-ch space, 1ch, *(sc, 3ch, sc) in corner space, (1ch, sc in space after next st) 6 times, 1ch; repeat from * 3 more times, join with a ss to first sc made. Fasten off.

Plain square

Size Crochet hook size F and medium-weight yarn produce a square 3in across (3 rounds worked).

Materials and uses Make a blanket from bulky wool or use chenille for a cushion cover.

Make 4ch
Round 1 (1dc, 1ch, 4dc, 1ch, 4dc, 1ch, 4dc, 1ch, 2dc) into the first ch st, ss into top of starting chain.
Round 2 3ch, dc into next dc, (2dc, 1ch, 2sc) into corner st ch, *4dc into 4dc, (2dc, 1ch, 2dc) into corner st; repeat from * twice more, 2dc, join with a ss. Continue in this way, working 1 dc into each dc and working the corners (1dc into corner st ch, 2dc, 1ch, 2dc), until square is the required size. Fasten off.

Wagon wheel

Size Crochet hook size E and medium-weight wool produce a square 3in across.

Materials and uses Join four or more for place mats, use individual squares as coasters.

This square uses 2 colors, A and B. Using A, make 6ch and join into a ring with a ss into first ch.
Round 1 2ch, 15dc in ring, join with ss in top of 2ch. Break off A.
Round 2 Join in B to ss, 4ch, *1dc in back loop only of next dc, 2ch; repeat from * to end of round, join with a ss to 2nd st of 4ch. Break off B.
Round 3 Join in A, 5ch, 1tr in same st, *2ch, 1dc in next dc, 2ch, 1hdc in next dc, 2ch, 1 dc in next dc, 2ch, (1tr, 2ch, 1tr) in next dc; repeat from * twice more, 2ch, 1dc in next dc, 2ch, 1 hdc in next dc, 2ch, 1dc in next dc, 2ch, join with a ss to 3rd st of 5ch.
Round 4 3sc in first space, 1sc in each st, 2sc in each space, 3sc in each corner space to end of round, join with a ss to first st. Fasten off.

Powder puff

Size Crochet hook size F and medium-weight yarn produce a square 2¾in across.
Materials and use Use machine-washable yarn for a carriage cover or baby's blanket, or use bulky yarn and a large hook for a rug.

This square uses 2 colors, A and B. Using A, make 6ch and join into a ring with a ss into first ch.
Round 1 1ch, 8sc into ring, join with a ss to first sc made.
Round 2 Pull up loop on hook to 1in, (yo, pull up loop in first sc to 1in) 4 times, yo and through all 9 loops on hook, 1ch tightly to fasten st (a puff st made), 4ch, *(yo, pull up loop in next sc to 1in) 4 times, yo and through all 9 loops on hook, 1ch

tightly, 2ch, make puff st same way in next sc, 4ch; repeat from * 2 more times, make puff st in last sc, 2ch, join with a ss to top of first puff st. Break off A.
Round 3 Join in B to any 4-ch corner space, 3ch, (2dc, 2ch, 3dc) in same space, *3dc in next space, (3dc, 2ch, 3dc) in next corner 4-ch space; repeat from * 2 times, 3dc in last space, join with a ss to 3rd ch of 3-ch. Fasten off.

Squares and triangles

Size Crochet hook size C and 3-ply wool produce a square 2in across.
Materials and uses Make a baby's blanket or shawl from fine, soft, machine-washable yarn, or use leftover medium-weight cotton for place mats.

This square uses 4 colors, A, B, C and D.
Round 1 Using A, make 4ch, 15dc into 4th ch from hook, join with a ss to top of 4ch. Break off A.
Round 2 Join in B to any st, 1sc into same place as join, (miss one st, 5hdc into next st, miss one st, 1sc into next st) 4 times omitting 1sc at end of last repeat, join with a ss to first sc. Break off B.
Round 3 Join in C to center hdc of any 5hdc group, 1sc into same place as join, (7dc into next sc, 1sc into center hdc of next 5hdc group) 4 times omitting 1sc at end of last repeat, join with a ss to first sc. Break off C.
Round 4 Join in D to center dc of any 7dc group, 1sc into same place as join, (9tr into next sc, 1sc into center dc of next 7dc group) 4 times omitting 1sc at end of last repeat, join with a ss to first sc. Fasten off.

Sea green square

Size Crochet hook size E and medium-weight yarn produce a square
3½in across.
Materials and uses Use leftover scraps of bulky or knitting worsted
for an afghan, or use medium-weight wool for cushion covers.

This square uses 4 colors, A, B, C
and D.
Using A, make 6ch and join into a
ring with a ss into first ch.
Round 1 3ch, 3dc into ring, (3ch,
4dc) 3 times into ring, 3ch, join with
a ss to 3rd of first 3ch. Break off A
and turn.
Round 2 (RS) Join in B to any 3ch
space, 3ch, 1dc into same space, (1dc
into each of next 4dc, 2dc into next
3ch space, 1dtr into commencing
circle between the 4dc groups, 2dc
into same space as last 2dc) 4 times
omitting 2dc at end of last repeat,
join with a ss to 3rd of first 3ch.
Break off B and turn.

Round 3 Join in C to any dtr, 3ch,
(1dc into each of next 8dc, 1dc, 3ch,
1dc into next dtr) 3 times, 1dc into
each of last 8dc, 1dc into same place
as join, 3ch, join with a ss to 3rd of
first 3ch. Break off C and turn.
Round 4 Join in D to any 3ch space,
3ch, 1dc into same space, (1dc into
each of next 10dc, 2dc into next 3ch
space, 1dtr around stem of dtr
worked on round 2 inserting hook
from right to left from front of work,
2dc into same space as last 2dc) 4
times, omitting 2dc at end of last
repeat, join with a ss to 3rd of first
3ch. Fasten off.

Irish lace square

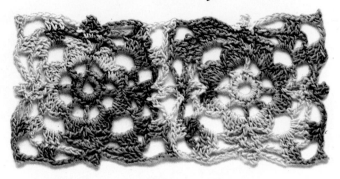

Size Crochet hook size 7 and very fine cotton produce a square 2in across.

Materials and uses Use fine or very fine cotton for tablecloth insertions or borders.

Make 8ch and join into a ring with a ss into first ch.

Round 1 1ch, 15sc into ring, join with a ss to first ch (16sc).

Round 2 5ch to count as first hdc and 3ch space, *miss 1sc, 1hdc into next sc, 3ch; repeat from * 6 more times, join with a ss to 2nd of first 5ch.

Round 3 (1sc, 1hdc, 3dc, 1hdc, 1sc) into each ch space to end, join with a ss to the first sc (8 petals).

Round 4 2ch to count as first hdc, *3ch, 1sc into 2nd dc of next petal, 6ch, 1sc into 2nd dc of next petal, 3ch, 1hdc into space before first sc of next petal, 3ch, 1hdc into same space; repeat from * twice more, 3ch, 1sc into 2nd dc of next petal, 6ch, 1sc into 2nd dc of next petal, 3ch, 1hdc into space before first sc of next petal, 3ch, join with a ss to 2nd of first 2ch.

Round 5 * 4ch, (3dc, 3ch, 3dc) into next 6ch space, 4ch, 1sc into hdc, 1sc into 3ch space, 1sc into hdc; repeat from * to end, join with a ss to first of first 4ch.

Round 6 * 5ch, 1dc into each of next 3dc, 5ch, insert hook into 3rd ch from hook and work 1sc to form picot, 2ch, 1dc into each of next 3dc, 5ch, ss into next sc, 4ch, insert hook into 3rd ch from hook and work 1sc to form picot, 1ch, miss 1sc, ss into next sc; repeat from * to end, join with a ss to first of first 5ch. Fasten off.

These squares may be crocheted together on the 6th round.

Rounds 1–5 As rounds 1–5 above.

Round 6 5ch, 1dc into each of next 3dc, 2ch, 1sc into corner picot of first square, 2ch, 1dc into each of next 3dc on 2nd square, ss into first of the 5ch after dc of first square, 4ch, ss into next sc of 2nd square, 1ch, 1sc into center side picot of first square, 1ch, miss 1sc on 2nd square, ss into next sc on 2nd square, 4ch, ss into ch before next 3dc on first square, 1dc into each of next 3dc on 2nd square, 2ch, 1sc into corner picot at end of first square, 2ch, complete round as for first square.

Subsequent squares may be joined in this way along one or more sides.

Square in a square

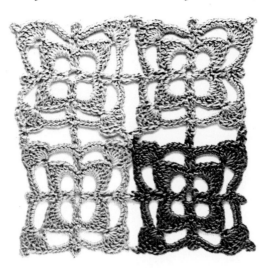

Size Crochet hook size C and fine cotton produce a square 2¾in across.

Material and uses Create a lacy bedspread from medium-weight cotton, or use silky yarn for cushion covers.

Make 8ch and join into a ring with a ss into first ch.

Round 1 3ch, 1dc in ring (6ch, 2dc in ring) 3 times, 6ch, join with a ss to top of 3ch.

Round 2 1sc between 3ch and dc, *(1sc, 1hdc, 2dc, 3tr, 2dc, 1hdc, 1sc) in next 6ch space, 1sc between next 2dc; repeat from * 3 more times, omitting 1sc at end of last repeat, join with a ss to first sc.

Round 3 Ss in next sc, 10ch, *miss next 4sts, 1sc in center tr, 7ch, miss next 4sts, 1dc in sc, miss next sc, 1dc in next sc, 7ch; repeat from * 3 more times, omitting 1dc and 7ch at end of last repeat, join with a ss to 3rd of 10ch.

Round 4 *6sc in ch space, 4tr in next sc, 5ch, ss in last st — 1pc worked —

3tr in same sc, 6sc in next ch space, 1sc between next 2dc, 1pc; repeat from * 3 more times, join with a ss to first sc. Fasten off.

These squares may be crocheted together on the 4th round.

Rounds 1–3 As rounds 1–3 above.

Round 4 * 6sc in ch space, 4tr in next sc, 2ch, ss in corner pc of first square, 2ch, ss in last st on 2nd square, 3tr in same sc, 6sc in next ch space, 1sc between next 2dc **, 2ch, ss to next pc of first square, 2ch, ss in last st on 2nd square; repeat from * to **, 1pc; repeat from * of round 4 of first square twice, join with a ss to first sc. Fasten off.

Subsequent squares may be joined in this way along one or more sides.

Lattice star

Size Crochet hook size 7 and fine cotton produce a square 4in across.
Materials and uses Make a tablecloth from fine cotton, or use very fine cotton for a tablecloth insertion or border.

Wind yarn 10 times around one finger, then slip loop off finger.
Round 1 32sc in ring, join with a ss.
Round 2 8ch, (1dc in next sc, miss 2sc, 1dc in next sc, 5ch) 7 times, 1dc in next sc, join with ss to 3rd of 8ch.
Round 3 *(3sc, 3ch, 3sc) in loop, 1sc between 2dc, 3ch, ss in last sc – pc worked; rep from * 7 more times, working last sc and pc between dc and 3ch, join with a ss to first sc.
Round 4 Ss to 3ch loop, 3ch, (4dc, 3ch, 5dc), *(5dc, 3ch, 5dc) in next 3ch loop; repeat from * 6 times, join with a ss to 3rd of 3ch.
Round 5 Ss to 3ch loop, 1sc in same loop, *8ch, (1tr, 7ch, 1tr) in next 3ch loop, 8ch, 1sc in next 3ch loop; repeat from * 3 more times, finishing last repeat ss in first sc.
Round 6 1sc in 1st sc, *pc, 8sc in ch

loop, 1sc in tr, pc, (5sc, pc, 4sc) in next ch loop, 1sc in tr, pc, 8sc in next ch loop, 1 sc in next sc; repeat from * 3 more times, finishing last repeat ss in first sc. Fasten off.
These squares may be crocheted together on the 6th round.
Rounds 1–5 As rounds 1–5 above.
Round 6 1sc in first sc, pc, 8sc in next lp, 1sc in next tr, pc, 5sc in next lp, then work 1ch, 1 sc in a corresponding pc on 1st square, 1ch, ss in last sc on 2nd square – joining pc worked – 4sc in same lp, 1sc in next tr, joining pc, 8sc in next lp, 1sc in next sc, joining pc, 8sc in next lp, 1sc in next tr, joining pc, 5sc in next lp, joining pc, 4sc in same lp, complete round as for first square.
Subsequent squares may be joined in this way along one or more sides.

Sparkle star

Size Crochet hook size C and medium-weight yarn produce a square 2¾in across.

Materials and uses Use lurex or other sparkling yarns for festive place mats and coasters, or make a lacy shawl from fine cotton.

This square uses 2 colors, A and B. Using A, make 4ch and join into a ring with a ss into first ch.

Round 1 1ch, 8sc into ring, join with a ss to first sc made.

Round 2 *6ch, sc in 3rd ch from hook, sc in next ch, hdc in each of next 2ch, ss in next sc on ring; repeat from * 7 more times. Break off A.

Round 3 Join in B to top of any petal, 5ch, dc in same space, *4ch, ss in top of next petal, 4ch, (dc, 2ch, dc) in top of next petal; repeat from * 2 times, 4ch, ss in top of last petal, 4ch, join with a ss to 3rd ch of 5-ch.

Round 4 *(3sc, 2ch, 3sc) in corner 2-ch space, 4sc in 4-ch space, miss ss, 4sc in next 4-ch space; repeat from * 3 times, join with a ss to first sc made.

Round 5 1ch, sc in joining st and in next 2sc, *3sc in corner 2-ch space, sc in each sc to next corner; repeat from * around, join with a ss to first sc made. Fasten off.

Diamond lattice

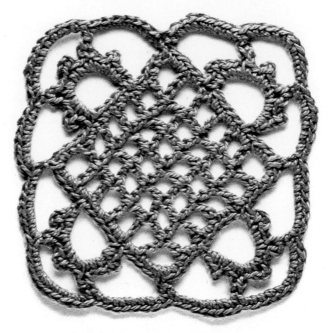

Size Crochet hook size E and medium-weight cotton produce a square 4¾in across.

Materials and uses Make a delicate tablecloth from multi-colored cotton, or use medium-weight cotton for pretty cushion covers.

Make 23ch.
Row 1 Into 8th ch from hook work 1dc, *2ch, miss 2ch, 1dc into next ch; repeat from * 4 more times, turn (6 spaces).
Row 2 5ch, 1dc into top of next dc, *2ch, 1dc into top of next dc; repeat from * 4 more times, turn.
Rows 3, 4, 5 and 6 As row 2.
Row 7 1ch, 2sc into space, *2sc into each of next 3 spaces, 10ch, turn, 1sc between sc immediately above 2nd dc in from left, turn, into 10ch loop work (2sc, 3ch) 5 times, 2sc into same loop, 2sc into next space to left,

6sc into corner; repeat from * 3 more times ending 3rd repeat with 3sc into corner instead of 6sc, join with a ss to first ch.
Row 8 1ch, *8ch, 1sc into 2nd of 3ch loop around circle, 10ch, 1sc into 4th of 3ch loop round circle, 8ch, 1sc between 3rd and 4th sc in corner space; repeat from * 3 more times, join with a ss to first ch.
Round 9 *8sc into 8ch loop, 10sc into 10ch loop, 8sc into 8ch loop; repeat from * 3 more times, join with a ss to first sc. Fasten off.

Lacy daisy

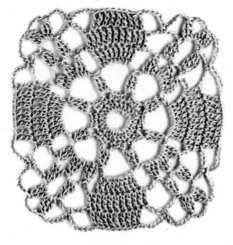

Size Crochet hook size E and medium-weight cotton produce a square 6¾in across.

Materials and uses Use medium-weight silky cotton for a bedspread, or fine cotton for a shawl.

Make 10ch and join into a ring with a ss into first ch.

Round 1 3ch, 23dc in ring, join.

Round 2 Sc in same place as ss, *3ch, sc in next 3sc; repeat from * around, ending with sc in last 2dc, join with a ss to first sc made.

Round 3 Ss in next 3-ch loop, 4ch, holding back on hook the last loop of each tr make 2tr in same 3-ch space, thread over and draw through all loops on hook − a 2-dc cluster made −, *7ch, holding back on hook the last loop of each tr make 3tr in next 3-ch and complete as for a cluster; repeat from * around, ending with 7ch, join with a ss to top of first cluster.

Round 4 Ss in 7-ch loop, 4ch, in same place as last ss make 2tr cluster, 4ch, 3tr cluster, 4ch and 3tr cluster; *4ch, 9tr in next 7-ch loop, 4ch, in next 7-ch loop make three 3tr clusters with 4ch between each cluster; repeat from * around, join last 4ch to top of first cluster.

Round 5 Ss in next 2ch, sc in 4-ch space, 4ch, 2tr cluster in last sc, *4ch, 3tr cluster in next 4-ch space, 7ch, tr in next space, tr in next 9tr, tr in next space, 7ch, 3tr cluster in next 4-ch space; repeat from * around, join last 7ch to top of first cluster.

Round 6 Ss in next loop, 4ch, 2tr cluster in same loop, *5ch, 3tr cluster in same loop, 7ch, sc in next loop, 7ch, miss 1 tr, tr in next 9tr, 7ch, sc in next loop, 7ch, 3tr cluster in next loop; repeat from * around, join and fasten off.

These squares may be crocheted together on the 6th round.

Rounds 1–5 As rounds 1–5 above

Round 6 Ss in next loop, 4ch, 2tr cluster in same loop, 2ch, ss in corresponding loop of first square, 2ch, 3tr cluster back in same place as last cluster on 2nd square, 3ch, sc in next loop on first square, 3ch, sc back in next loop on 2nd square, 3ch, sc in next loop on first square, 3ch, miss 1tr on 2nd square, tr in next 4tr, ss in 5th tr on first square, tr in next 5tr back on 2nd square, and continue as for first square, joining next 3 loops to corresponding loops of first square as first 3 loops were joined. Complete round as for first square. Subsequent squares may be joined in this way along one or more sides.

Petal square

Size Crochet hook size E and medium-weight wool produce a square 2½in across.

Materials and uses Use odds and ends of yarn to make a multi-colored blanket, or make a delicate shawl from fine or medium-weight cotton.

This square uses 4 colors, A, B, C and D.

Using A, make 4ch and join into a ring with a ss into first ch.

Round 1 4ch, (dc in ring, 1ch) 7 times, join with a ss to 3rd ch of 4-ch. Break off A (8 spaces around).

Round 2 Join in B to any 1-ch space, 3ch, make cluster st in same space, (yo, pull up loop in space, yo and through 2 loops on hook) 3 times, yo and through all 4 loops on hook, 1ch tightly, 2ch, *make cluster st in next 1-ch space (yo, pull up loop in space, yo and through 2 loops on hook) 4 times, yo and through all 5 loops on hook, 1ch tightly, 2ch; repeat from * 6 more times, join with a ss to top of first cluster st. Break off B.

Round 3 Join in C to any 2-ch space, (3ch, 2dc, 2ch, 3dc) in same space, *3dc in next space, (3dc, 2ch, 3dc) in next space; repeat from * 2 more times, 3dc in last space, join with a ss to 3rd ch of 3-ch. Break off C.

Round 4 Join in D to any dc on any side of square, sc in same st and in every st till 2-ch corner space, *(sc, 2ch, sc) in corner, sc in every st till next corner 2-ch space; repeat from * around, join with a ss to first sc made. Fasten off.

Flower square

Size Crochet hook size G and knitting worsted produce a square 6¾in across.

Materials and uses Make a bedspread from medium-weight cotton, or sew four squares together to make a cushion cover.

This square uses 2 colors, A and B.
Note *Cluster (cl): Work 3dc keeping last loop of each st on hook, draw a loop through all sts on hook.*
Using A, make 6ch and join into a ring with a ss into first ch.
Round 1 2ch, 23dc into ring, join with a ss to 2nd of 2ch.
Round 2 4ch, 1dc into same ch as ss, 1ch, *miss 2sts, (1dc, 2ch, 1dc) into next st, 1ch; repeat from * 6 more times, join with a ss to 2nd of 4ch.
Round 3 2ch, (1dc, 2ch, 2dc) into first ch space, *1sc into 1ch space, (2dc, 2ch, 2dc) into 2ch space; repeat from * 6 more times, 1sc into last ch space. Break off A.

Round 4 Join in B to next 2ch space with a sc, *7ch, 1sc into next 2ch space, 5ch, 1sc into next 2ch space; repeat from * 3 more times ending with a ss into joining sc instead of sc.
Round 5 2ch, *7dc into 7ch loop (2ch, 1cl, 3ch, 1cl, 2ch) into 5ch loop; repeat from * 3 more times, join with a ss to 2nd of 2ch.
Round 6 2ch, *1dc into each dc, 2dc into 2ch loop, (2ch, 1cl, 3ch, 1cl, 2ch) into 3ch loop, 2dc into 2ch loop; repeat from * 3 more times, join with a ss to 2nd of 2ch.
Round 7 As round 6 but ending 1dc into each of last 2dc, join with a ss to 2nd of 2ch. Fasten off.

Lacy shells

Size Crochet hook size D and fine cotton produce a square 3¼in across (measured diagonally).

Materials and uses Make matching place mats and coasters from medium-weight cotton.

Make 10ch and join into a ring with a ss into first ch.

Round 1 7ch, *5tr into ring, 3ch; repeat from * 2 times, 4tr into ring, join with a ss to 4th ch of 7-ch.

Round 2 Ss into corner space, 5ch, (tr, 1ch) 7 times into same space, *(tr, 1ch) 8 times into next corner space; repeat from * twice, join with a ss to 4th ch of 5-ch.

Round 3 1ch, sc in same st, sc in next 1-ch space, *sc in next tr, (sc, 1ch, sc) in next 1-ch space, (sc in next tr, sc in next 1-ch space) 3 times, sc in next tr, (sc, 1ch, sc) in next 1-ch space, (sc in next tr, sc in next 1-ch space) 3 times; repeat from * around, join with a ss to first sc made. Fasten off.

To join Sew corners of squares together.

Lattice square

Size Crochet hook size E and knitting worsted produce a square 3¼in across.
Materials and uses Use a large crochet hook and thick string to make a hard-wearing door mat, or make a blanket from tweedy bouclé yarn.

This square uses 3 colors, A, B and C.
Row 1 Using A, 12ch, dc in 6th ch from hook, *1ch, miss 1ch, dc in next ch; repeat from * 2 times, 4ch, turn.
Row 2 Dc in 2nd dc, *1ch, dc in next dc; repeat from * once, 1ch, dc in 2nd ch on 6-ch loop, 4ch, turn.
Row 3 *Dc in next dc, 1ch; repeat from * 2 times, work last dc in 2nd ch of 4-ch, 4ch, turn.
Row 4 As row 3. Break off A.

Round 1 Join in B to any corner space, (3ch, 2dc, 3ch, 3dc) in same space, *3dc in each of next 2 spaces, (3dc, 3ch, 3dc) in next corner space; repeat from * 2 times, 3dc in each of last 2 spaces, join with a ss to 3rd ch of 3-ch. Break off B.
Round 2 Join in C to any 3-ch corner space, (sc, 2ch, sc) in same space, *sc in every dc to next corner, (sc, 2ch, sc) in next corner 3-ch space; repeat from * around, join with a ss to first sc made. Fasten off.

Afghan square

Size Crochet hook size D and medium-weight yarn produce a square 3¼in across.

Materials and uses Make a brightly colored afghan from scraps of knitting worsted or bulky yarn, or use machine-washable yarn in pretty pastel shades for a baby's blanket.

This square uses 5 colors, A, B, C, D and E.

Using A make 4ch and join into a ring with a ss into first ch.

Round 1 3ch, 2dc into ring, (2ch, 3dc into ring) 3 times, 2ch, join with a ss to 3rd of first 3ch. Break off A.

Round 2 Join in B to any 2ch space, 3ch, 2dc, 2ch, 3dc into 2ch space, (1ch, 3dc, 2ch, 3dc into next 2ch space) 3 times, 1ch, join with a ss to 3rd of first 3ch. Break off B.

Round 3 Join in C to corner 2ch space, 3ch, 2dc, 2ch, 3dc into 2ch space, (1ch, 3dc into next 1ch space, 1ch, 3dc, 2ch, 3dc into next 2ch space) 3 times, 1ch, 3dc into next 1ch space, 1ch, join with a ss to 3rd of

first 3ch. Break off C.

Round 4 Join in D to corner 2ch space, 3ch, 2dc, 2ch, 3dc into 2ch space, *(1 ch, 3dc into next 1ch space) twice, 1ch, 3dc, 2ch, 3dc into next 2ch space; repeat from * 3 more times, (1ch, 3dc into next 1ch space) twice, 1ch, join with a ss to 3rd of first 3ch. Break off D.

Round 5 Join in E to corner 2ch space, 3ch, 2dc, 2ch, 3dc into 2ch space, *(1ch, 3dc into next 1ch space) 3 times, 1ch, 3dc, 2ch, 3dc into next 2ch space; repeat from * 3 more times (1ch, 3dc into next 1ch space) 3 times, 1ch, join with a ss to 3rd of first 3ch. Fasten off.

HEXAGONS

As with square designs, hexagons can be joined together to create a solid fabric, so they are particularly suitable for warm afghans and blankets. By making use of leftover scraps of yarn a patchwork effect can be achieved with the Tinkerbell *pattern, p.47.*

Ribbed hexagon

Size Crochet hook size E and crêpe cotton produce a hexagon 3½in across (6 rounds worked).

Materials and uses Make a cushion cover from slub linen or cotton yarn, or use thick cotton for place mats and coasters.

Make 4ch and join into a ring with a ss into first ch.

Round 1 3ch to count as first dc, (1dc, 1ch, 1dc) 5 times into ring, 1dc into ring, 1ch, join with a ss to 3rd of first 3ch (12dc).

Round 2 Ss into first dc and first ch space, 4ch to count as first dc and 1ch space, 1dc into same place as last ss, inserting hook from back to front work 1dc round stem of next dc — called 1dc back —, 1dc back into next dc, *(1dc, 1ch, 1dc) into next 1ch space, 1dc back into each of next 2dc; repeat from * 4 more times, (1dc, 1ch, 1dc) into last 1ch space, 1dc back round first 3ch of round 1, 1dc back round first dc of round 1, join with a ss to 3rd of first 4ch (24dc).

Round 3 Ss into first 1ch space, 4ch to count as first dc and 1ch space, 1dc into same 1ch space, *1dc back into each of next 4dc, (1dc, 1ch, 1dc) into next 1ch space; repeat from * 4 more times, 1dc back into each of next 4 sts, join with a ss to 3rd of first 4ch (36dc). Continue in this way, increasing 12 dc on each round, working 1dc back into each dc on sides and (1dc, 1ch, 1dc) into each 1ch space at corners until hexagon is the required size. Fasten off.

Blue belle

Size Crochet hook size C and medium-weight wool produce a hexagon 3¼in across.

Materials and uses Make an afghan from leftover bulky or knitting worsted, or use lurex and chenille for a novelty cushion.

This design uses 3 colors, A, B and C.

Using A, make 4ch and join into a ring with a ss into first ch.

Round 1 3ch, yarn over hook, insert hook in ring and draw loop out to length of 3-ch, yarn over hook and draw through all 3 loops on hook − a long hdc made −, make 16 more long hdc in ring, join with a ss to top of 3-ch. Break off A.

Round 2 Join in B, 1ch and, working through the 2 back loops only of each long hdc, make sc in each st around, thus forming a ridge on right side (36sc in round), join by inserting hook in first sc made and drawing through a loop of C. Do not break off B.

Round 3 Working over B with C,

make 4ch, 3tr in base of ch, *drop C (do not work over it) and, with B, yarn over hook twice and, holding back on hook the last loop of each tr, make tr in same place as C trs and in each of next 6 sts, drop B and, with C, yarn over hook and draw through all 8 loops on hook − a cluster made −, working over B, make 7 C tr in same place as last B tr of cluster; repeat from * around, ending with C, 3tr in same place as last tr of cluster, join with a ss to top of 4-ch. Break off B.

Round 4 3ch, dc in same place as ss, 2ch, 2dc in same place, *dc in next 7 sts, in next st make 2dc, 2ch and 2 dc; repeat from * around, join with a ss to top of 3-ch. Fasten off.

Tinkerbell

Size Crochet hook size E and medium-weight yarn produce a hexagon 2¾in across.

Materials and uses Make a baby's blanket from machine-washable medium-weight crêpe, or use bulky yarn for an afghan.

This hexagon uses 4 colors, A, B, C and D.

Using A, make 5ch and join into a ring with a ss into first ch.

Round 1 3ch, 1dc in ring, *1ch, 2dc in ring; repeat from * 4 more times, 1ch, join with a ss to top of 3-ch. Break off A.

Round 2 Join in B to first 1-ch space, 3ch, (1dc, 1ch, 2dc) in same space, 1ch, *(2dc, 1ch, 2dc) for shell in next 1-ch space, 1ch; repeat from * 4 more times, join with a ss to top of 3-ch. Break off B.

Round 3 Join in C to 1-ch space of first shell, 3ch, (1dc, 1ch, 2dc) in same space, *1ch, 2dc in 1-ch space between shells, 1ch, (2dc, 1ch, 2dc) in 1-ch space of next shell; repeat from * 4 times, 1ch, 2dc in next 1-ch space, ss in top of 3ch. Break off C.

Round 4 Join in D to 1-ch space of first shell, 1ch, 1sc in each dc and each 1-ch space between shells, 2sc in each 1-ch space of shells, join with a ss to first 1-ch. Fasten off.

Anemone

Size Crochet hook size C and medium-weight cotton produce a hexagon 3in across.

Materials and uses Make a shawl for special occasions from mohair or angora, or use thick bouclé or terry-mix cotton for a bath mat.

This hexagon uses 4 colors, A, B, C and D.

Using A, make 9ch and join into a ring with a ss into first ch.

Round 1 1ch, 18sc into ring, join with a ss to first sc made. Break off A.

Round 2 Join in B to any sc, 3ch, dc in each of next 2sc, 6ch, *dc in each of next 3sc, 6ch; repeat from * 4 more times, join with a ss to 3rd ch of 3-ch. Break off B.

Round 3 Join in C to first dc of any 3-dc group, 3ch, 2dc in next dc, dc in 3rd dc, 4ch, *in next 3-dc group

work dc in first dc, 2dc in second dc, dc in 3rd dc, 4ch; repeat from * 4 more times, join with a ss to 3rd ch of 3-ch. Break off C.

Round 4 Join in D to first dc of any 4-dc group, 3ch, dc in each of next 3dc, 3ch, sc loosely over the 2 chain loops below, 3ch, *dc in each of next 4dc, 3ch, sc loosely over the 2 chain loops below, 3ch; repeat from * 4 more times, join with a ss to third ch of 3-ch. Fasten off.

To join Sew together the 4-dc edges only.

Pinwheel

Size Crochet hook size C and medium-weight cotton produce a hexagon 2½in across.

Materials and uses Create a baby's blanket or carriage cover from leftover medium-weight yarn, or use bulky yarn for a cushion cover.

This hexagon uses 4 colors, A, B, C and D.

Using A, make 5ch and join into a ring with ss into first ch.

Round 1 6ch, (dc in ring, 3ch) 5 times, 3ch, join with a ss to 3rd ch of 6-ch. Break off A.

Round 2 Join in B to any dc, pull up loop on hook to 1in, *(yo, insert hook under the dc st and pull through a 1in loop) 4 times, yo and through all loops on hook, 1ch tightly, (puff st made), 5ch; repeat from * 5 times, working under every dc st around, including the 3-ch, join with a ss to top of first puff st. Break off B.

Round 3 Join in C to any 5-ch space, 3ch, (2dc, 2ch, 3dc) in same space, *(3dc, 2ch, 3dc) in next space; repeat from * 4 times, join with a ss to 3rd ch of 3-ch. Break off C.

Round 4 Join in D to any 2-ch space, (sc, 2ch, sc) in same space, *sc in every dc till next corner 2-ch space, (sc, 2ch, sc) in 2-ch space; repeat from * 4 times, sc in every remaining st, join with a ss to first sc made. Fasten off.

Ornate hexagon

Size Crochet hook size C and fine cotton produce a hexagon 3¾in across.

Materials and uses Use fine cotton for an appliqué motif for a cushion, or make a matching luncheon set from medium-weight cotton.

This hexagon uses 2 colors, A and B. Using A, wind yarn 20 times round one finger, then slip loop off finger. Catch ring together with a ss.

Round 1 4ch, 4tr into ring, (2ch, 5tr into ring) 5 times, 2ch, join with a ss to top of 4ch at beginning of round. Break off A.

Round 2 Join in B to any 2ch space, 2sc into same space, (9ch, 2sc into next space) 6 times omitting last 2sc, join with a ss to beginning of round.

Round 3 (1sc into each of next 2sc, 13sc into 9ch loop) 6 times, join with a ss to beginning of round.

Round 4 Ss into each of next 5sc, (1sc into each of next 7sc, 9ch, miss next 8sc) 6 times.

Round 5 *1sc into each sc of next group, (3ch, ss to top of last sc − picot made −, 2sc into 9ch loop) 4 times, 3ch, ss to top of last sc; repeat from * all around. Fasten off.

Spoked hexagon

Size Crochet hook size D and medium-weight wool produce a hexagon 4½in across (7 rounds worked).

Materials and uses Make cushion covers from medium-weight wool, or use cotton crêpe for place mats and coasters.

Make 5ch and join into a ring with a ss into first ch.

Round 1 4ch to count as first dc, and 1ch space, (2ch, 1ch) 5 times into ring, 1dc into ring, join with a ss to 3rd of first 3ch (12dc).

Round 2 3ch to count as first dc, *2dc into next 1ch space, 1dc into next dc, 2ch, 1dc into next dc; repeat from * 4 more times, 1dc into next dc, 2ch, join with a ss to 3rd of first 3ch (24dc).

Round 3 3ch to count as first dc, 1dc at base of 3ch, *1dc into each of next 2dc, 2dc into next dc, 3ch, 2dc into next dc; repeat from * 4 more times, 1dc into each of next 2dc, 2dc into next dc, 3ch, join with a ss to 3rd of first 3ch (36dc).

Round 4 3ch to count as first dc, 1dc at base of 3ch, *1dc into each of next 4dc, 2dc into next dc, 3ch, 2dc into next dc; repeat from * 4 more times, 1dc into each of next 4dc, 2dc into next dc, 3ch, join with a ss to 3rd of first 3ch (48dc).

Continue in this way, increasing 12dc on each round, working 3ch at each corner, until hexagon is the required size. Fasten off.

Little spindles

Size Crochet hook size D and crêpe cotton produce a hexagon 2½in across.

Materials and uses For place mats join together seven hexagons made from medium-weight yarn, or use washable yarn for a baby's afghan.

Make 6ch and join into a ring with a ss into first ch.

Round 1 5ch, (tr in ring, 2ch) 11 times, join with a ss to 3rd ch of 5-ch (12 spaces).

Round 2 Ss into next 2-ch space, (3ch, dc, 2ch, 2dc) in same space, 3dc in next space, *(2dc, 2ch, 2dc) in next space, 3dc in next space; repeat from * 4 more times, join with a ss to 3rd ch of 3-ch. Fasten off.

Snowflake

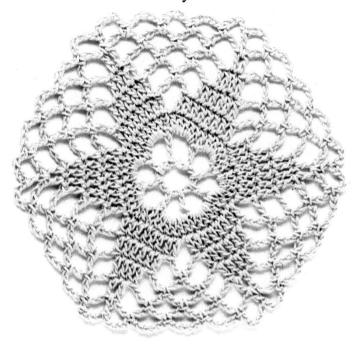

Size Crochet hook size C and fine cotton produce a hexagon 5¼in across.

Materials and uses Make a tablecloth from fine or medium-weight cotton, or make a shawl from fine angora.

Make 12 ch and join into a ring with a ss into first ch.

Round 1 7ch (to count as dc and 4ch), dc in ring, (4ch, dc in ring) 6 times, 4ch, join with ss to 3rd of 7ch.

Round 2 3ch (to count as dc), *5dc in next sp, dc in next dc; rep from * around, join with ss to top of 3ch.

Round 3 3ch, dc in next 7dc, 5ch, *dc in next 8dc, 5ch; repeat from * around, join (6 groups of dc with 5ch between groups).

Round 4 Ss in next dc, 3ch, dc in next 5dc, *5ch, sc in lp, 5ch, miss 1dc, dc in next 6dc; rep from * around, end with 5ch, sc in lp, 5ch, join.

Round 5 Ss in next dc, 3ch, dc in next 3dc, *(5ch, sc in next loop) twice, 5ch, miss 1dc, dc in next 4dc; repeat from * around, join.

Round 6 Ss in next dc, 3ch, dc in next dc, *(5ch, sc in next loop) 3 times, 5ch, miss 1dc, dc in next 2dc; repeat from * around, join.

Round 7 Ss between 3ch and dc, 8ch *(sc in next loop, 5ch) 4 times, dc between next 2dc, 5ch; repeat from * around, join last 5ch to 3rd st of 8ch. Fasten off. These hexagons may be crocheted together on the 7th round.

Rounds 1–6 As rounds 1–6 above.

Round 7 Ss between 3ch and dc, 8ch, (sc in next loop, 5ch) 4 times, dc between next 2dc, (2ch, sc in corresponding loop on first hexagon, 2ch, sc in next loop on 2nd hexagon) 4 times, 2ch, sc in next loop on first hexagon, 2ch, dc between next 2dc on 2nd hexagon, complete round as for 1st hexagon.

Subsequent hexagons may be joined in this way along one or more sides.

Rosette

Size Crochet hook size C and fine cotton produce a motif 2in across.
Materials and uses Join together seven motifs made from different shades of medium-weight cotton for pretty place mats, or use bulky cotton yarn for a bedspread.

This design uses 2 colors, A and B. Using A, make 9ch and join into a ring with a ss into first ch.
Round 1 3ch, 2dc in ring, *6ch, ss sideways in last dc made, 3dc in ring; repeat from * 4 times, 6ch, ss in last dc, ss in 3rd ch of 3-ch. Break off A.
Round 2 Join in B to any center dc of any 3-dc group, *work 11dc sts into 6-ch loop, ss in center dc of next 3-dc group; repeat from * 5 more times, ss in st where yarn was attached.
Fasten off.
To join Sew top edge stitches of petals together.

Hidden petals

Size Crochet hook size B and fine cotton produce a hexagon 3in across.

Materials and uses Make a tablecloth from fine, washable cotton, or use silky yarn to make a luxurious evening shawl.

Make 6ch and join into a ring with a ss into first ch.

Round 1 3ch, 11dc in ring, join with a ss to 3rd ch of 3-ch.

Round 2 3ch, dc in joining, 2dc in next dc, *1ch, 2dc in each of next 2dc; repeat from * 4 times, 1ch, join with a ss to 3rd ch of 3-ch.

Round 3 3ch, dc in joining, dc in each of next 2dc, 2dc in 3rd dc, *2ch, miss 1ch, 2dc in next dc, dc in each of next 2dc, 2dc in next dc; repeat from * 4 times, 2ch, join with a ss to 3rd ch of 3-ch.

Round 4 3ch, dc in joining, dc in each of next 4dc, 2dc in last dc of section, *3ch, 2dc in first dc of next section, dc in each of next 4dc, 2dc in last dc of section; repeat from * 4 times, 3ch, join with a ss to 3rd ch of 3-ch.

Round 5 3ch, dc in joining, dc in each of next 6dc, 2dc in last dc of section, *4ch, 2dc in first dc of next section, dc in each of next 6dc, 2dc in last dc of section; repeat from * 4 times, 4ch, join with a ss to 3rd ch of 3-ch. Fasten off.

To join Arrange hexagons as illustrated and sew dc stitches of adjoining medallions together, not the chain loops.

Flower hexagon

Size Crochet hook size D and medium-weight cotton produce a hexagon 4¾in across (6 rounds worked).
Materials and uses Use bulky yarn for cushion covers.

Make 6ch and join into a ring with a ss into first ch.
Round 1 3ch, leaving last loop of each dc on hook work 2dc into ring, yo and draw through all 3 loops on hook − called 2dc cluster −, *3ch, leaving last loop of each dc on hook work 3dc into ring, yo and draw through all 4 loops on hook − called 3dc cluster −; repeat from * 4 more times, 1ch, 1hdc into top of 2dc cluster (6 clusters).
Round 2 3ch, 2dc cluster into side of hdc just worked, *3ch, (3dc cluster, 3ch, 3dc cluster) into next 3ch loop; repeat from * ending 3ch, 3dc into top of hdc on previous round, 1ch, 1hdc into 3rd of first 3ch (12 clusters).
Round 3 3ch to count as first dc, 2dc cluster into top of hdc just worked, *3ch, (3dc cluster, 3ch, 3dc cluster) into next 3ch loop, 3ch, 3dc cluster into next 3ch loop; repeat from * 4 times, 3ch, (3dc cluster, 3ch, 3dc

cluster) into next 3ch lp, 1ch, 1hdc into 3rd of first 3ch (18 clusters).
Round 4 3ch, 1dc into side of hdc just worked, 2dc into next 3ch loop, *(2dc, 2ch, 2dc) into next 3ch loop, (2dc into next 3ch loop) twice; repeat from * 4 times, (2dc, 2ch, 2dc) into next 3ch lp, join with ss to 3rd of 1st 3ch (48dc).
Round 5 3ch to count as first dc, 1dc into each of next 5dc, *3dc into next 2ch space, 1dc into each of next 8dc; repeat from * 4 times, 3dc into next 2ch space, 1dc into each of next 2dc, join with ss to top of first 3ch (66dc).
Round 6 3ch to count as first dc, 1dc into each of next 6dc, *3dc into next dc, 1dc into each of next 10dc; repeat from * 4 more times, 3dc into next dc, 1dc into each of next 3dc, join with a ss to top of first 3ch (78dc).
Continue in this way, increasing 12dc on each round, working 3dc into each dc at corners, until hexagon is the required size. Fasten off.

Afghan hexagon

Size Crochet hook size D and medium-weight wool produce a hexagon 4¾in across (7 rounds worked).

Materials and uses Use scraps of medium-weight yarn or knitting worsted for a multi-colored blanket, or make a shawl from silky yarn or wool crêpe.

This hexagon uses 2 colors, A and B. Using A, make 4ch and join into a ring with a ss into first ch.

Round 1 1ch, 12sc into ring, join with a ss to first ch (12sc).

Round 2 5ch to count as first dc and 2ch space, *(1dc, 2ch) into next sc; repeat from * to end, join with a ss to 3rd of first 5ch (12 2-ch spaces). Break off A.

Round 3 Join in B with a ss into first 2ch space, 3ch, leaving last loop of each dc on hook work 3dc into next 2ch space, yo and draw through all 4 loops on hook − first cluster worked −, *3ch, leaving last loop of each dc on hook work 4dc into next 2ch space, yo and draw through all 5 loops on hook; repeat from * ending 3ch, join with a ss to 3rd of first 3ch. Break off B.

Round 4 Join in A with a ss into top of first cluster and first ch of first 3ch loop, 3ch to count as first dc, 3dc into same loop, *1ch, 4 dc into next 3ch loop; repeat from * ending 1ch, join with a ss to 3rd of first 3ch (48dc). Break off A.

Round 5 Join in B with a ss into first 3dc and 1ch space, 3ch to count as first dc, (2dc, 2ch, 3dc) into first 1ch space, *2ch, 4dc into next 1ch space, 2ch, (3dc, 2ch, 3dc) into next 1ch space; repeat from * 4 more times, 2ch, 4dc into next 1ch space, 2ch, join with a ss to 3rd of first 3ch (1 group of 4dc on each edge). Break off B.

Round 6 Join in A with a ss into first 2dc, 3ch to count as first dc, (2dc, 2ch, 3dc) into first 2ch space, *2ch, (4dc into next 2ch space, 2ch) twice, (3dc, 2ch, 3dc) into next 2ch space; repeat from * 4 more times, 2ch, (4dc into next 2ch space, 2ch) twice, join with a ss to 3rd of first 3ch (2 groups of 4dc on each edge). Break off A. Continue in this way, increasing 1 group of 4dc on each edge, working (3dc, 2ch, 3dc) into each 2ch space at the corners until hexagon is the required size. Fasten off.

Cobweb

Size Crochet hook size D and medium-weight yarn produce a design 3¼in across.

Materials and uses Use fine silky cotton or mohair glitter yarn to create a luxurious evening shawl, or use bulky cotton for place mats and coasters.

Make 4ch and join into a ring with a ss into first ch.

Round 1 3ch, 17dc in ring, join with a ss to top of 3ch.

Round 2 *5ch, miss 2 sts, 1sc in next st; repeat from * 4 more times, 5ch, 1sc in first st of 5ch.

Round 3 *7ch, 1sc in next sc; repeat from * 4 more times, 7ch, 1sc in first st of 7ch.

Round 4 *9ch, 1sc in next sc; repeat from * 4 more times, 9ch, 1sc in first st of 9ch.

Round 5 *11ch, 1sc in next sc; repeat from * 4 more times, 11ch, 1sc in first st of 11ch.

Round 6 *13ch, 1sc in next sc; repeat from * 4 more times, 13ch, 1sc in first st of 13ch. Fasten off.

TRIANGLES

Triangular motifs can be combined with hexagons to make even more interesting designs, or they can be used on their own. Their shape makes them particularly suitable for making shawls or headscarves, but they can of course be used for virtually any crochet project.

Lace triangle

Size Crochet hook size C and fine cotton produce a triangle with sides 2¼in long.

Materials and uses Join several made from medium-weight yarn for place mats and coasters, or use thick cotton for a bedspread.

This triangle uses 3 colors, A, B and C.

Using A, make 6ch and join into a ring with a ss into first ch.

Round 1 4ch, (dc in ring, 1 ch) 11 times, join with a ss to 3rd ch of 4-ch. Break off A.

Round 2 Join in B to any 1-ch space, 4ch, ★ (tr, 7ch, tr) in next space, (1ch, dc in next space) 3 times, 1ch; repeat from ★ once more, (tr, 7ch, tr) in next space, (1ch, dc in next space) 2 times, 1ch, join with a ss to 3rd ch of 4-ch. Break off B.

Round 3 Join in C to the 1-ch space before any corner tr, sc in same space, ★ 1ch, (sc, 1ch, sc, 5ch, sc, 1ch, sc) in corner 7-ch space, (1ch, sc in next 1-ch space) 4 times; repeat from ★ once more, 1ch, (sc, 1ch, sc, 5ch, sc, 1ch, sc) in next space, (1ch, sc in next 1-ch space) 3 times, 1ch, join with a ss to first sc made. Fasten off.

Shell triangle

Size Crochet hook size F and knitting worsted produce a triangle with sides 3¼in long.
Materials and uses Use scraps of brightly colored knitting worsted

to make a cushion cover, or make a bedspread from bulky wool or cotton.

This triangle uses 3 colors, A, B and C.

Using A, make 4ch and join into a ring with a ss into first ch.

Round 1 3ch to count as 1dc, 11dc into ring, join with a ss into top of 3ch.

Round 2 (5ch, ss into 4th dc of previous round) twice, 5ch, join with ss. Break off A.

Round 3 Join in B into first 5ch space, 3ch to count as 1dc, 6dc, 2ch, (7dc 2ch) twice, join to top of 3ch. Break off B.

Round 4 Join in C to any 2ch space, 3ch, 8dc into 2ch space, 7sc, (9dc into 2ch space, 7sc) twice, ss into top of first 3ch. Fasten off.

Eternal triangle

Size Crochet hook size D and medium-weight yarn produce a triangle with sides 3½in long.
Materials and uses Make potholders from leftover knitting worsted or bulky yarn, or use bulky cotton for coasters.

Make 4ch and join into a ring with a ss into first ch.

Round 1 3ch to count as 1dc, 11dc into ring, join with a ss into 3rd of first 3ch.

Round 2 (5ch, ss into 4th dc of previous round) twice, 5ch, join with a ss to base of first 5ch.

Round 3 Ss into 5ch sp, 3ch to count as 1dc, 6dc, 2ch, (7dc, 2ch) twice, join to top of 3ch.

Round 4 2ch, 6hdc, 9dc in 2ch sp, (7hdc, 9dc in 2ch sp) twice, ss in top of 2ch.

Round 5 4ch, (miss hdc, 1dc, 1ch,) 5 times, *1dc, in next dc, 4ch, miss 1dc, 1dc in next dc, 1ch, 1dc, (1ch, miss 1dc, 1dc), 6 times, 1ch, repeat from * once more, 1dc, 4ch, miss 1dc, 1dc, 1ch, 1dc, 1ch, ss in 3rd ch at start.

Round 6 3ch, 1dc in 1ch sp, 1dc in each dc to 4ch sp, 3dc, 2ch, 3dc, into corner sp, all round, ss in top of 3ch. Fasten off.

Crossed triangle

Size Crochet hook size D and medium-weight cotton produce a triangle with sides 6½in long.

Materials and uses Join together two large triangles made from bulky yarn for a novelty cushion cover, or make coasters from medium-weight cotton.

Make 6ch and join into a ring with a ss into first ch.

Round 1 2ch, *into ring work 3dc but keep last loop of each dc on hook, then draw a loop through all loops on hook − called 1 cluster −, 5ch; repeat from * twice more.

Round 2 *1sc into cluster, 3ch, (3dc, 3ch, 3dc, 3ch) into ch loop of previous round; repeat from * twice more.

Round 3 1sc into ch loop, 3ch, (3dc, 3ch, 3dc, 3ch) into ch loop between 3dc groups, (1sc, 3ch) into next 2ch loops; repeat from * twice more.

Round 4 *1dc into each dc, (2dc, 3ch, 2dc) into ch loop, 1dc into each dc, 3ch, 1dc into next ch loop, 1 cluster into next ch loop, 1dc into next ch loop, 3ch; repeat from * twice more.

Round 5 *1dc into each dc (2dc, 3ch, 2dc) into ch loop, 1dc into each dc, 3ch, 1sc into next ch loop, 3ch, 1sc into next ch loop, 3ch; repeat from * twice more.

Round 6 As round 4.

Round 7 As round 5.

Round 8 * 1 sc into each dc, 3sc into corner ch loop, 1sc into each dc, (1sc into ch loop) 3 times; repeat from * twice more, join with a ss, work 1 ch then work another row of sc right around, but working from left to right instead of from right to left. Fasten off.

Tricorn

Size Crochet hook size F and knitting worsted produce a triangle with
sides 3½in long.

Materials and uses Use leftover bulky yarn in bright colors for a
blanket, or use subtle shades of medium-weight cotton for a cushion
cover.

This triangle uses 4 colors, A, B, C
and D.

Using A, make 4ch and join into a
ring with a ss into first ch.

Round 1 3ch, 11dc in ring, join with
a ss to 3rd ch of 3-ch. Break off A.

Round 2 Join in B to any dc, 3ch, 4dc
in same st, *hdc in next st, sc in next
st, dc in next st, 5dc in 4th st; repeat
from * once more, hdc, sc, dc, join
with a ss to 3rd ch of 3-ch. Break
off B.

Round 3 Join in C to 3rd dc of any 5-
dc corner, 3ch, 4dc in same st, *hdc
in each of next 7 sts, 5dc in 8th st;
repeat from * around, join with a ss
to 3rd ch of 3-ch. Break off C.

Round 4 Join in D to middle dc of
any 5-dc corner, 1ch, (2sc, 1ch, 2sc)
in same st, *sc in every st till next
corner's middle dc st, (2sc, 1ch, 2sc)
in that st; repeat from * around, join
with a ss to first sc made. Fasten off.

CIRCLES & OCTAGONS

When circular or octagonal designs are joined together, there will be spaces between the various elements. These spaces may be filled with small filler motifs (see pp. 79–84), or they may be left as they are to create a delicate, lacy fabric.

Many of the more solid designs in this chapter can easily be made into cushions by working more rounds until the medallion is the required size.

Plain circle

Size Crochet hook size F and cotton crêpe produce a circle 5in across (5 rounds worked).

Materials and uses Make cushions from knitting worsted or bulky yarn, or use medium-weight or crêpe cotton for place mats and coasters.

Make 3ch and join into a ring with a ss into first ch.

Round 1 3ch, 15dc into ring, join with a ss into top of first ch.

Round 2 3ch, 2dc into each dc to end, join with a ss into top of first ch.

Round 3 3ch, *2dc into next dc, 1dc; repeat from * around, join with a ss into first ch.

Round 4 3ch, *dc into first dc, 2dc, repeat from * around, join with a ss into first ch.

Round 5 3ch, *dc into first dc, 3dc, repeat from * around, join with a ss into first ch. Fasten off.

Lemon and lime

Size Crochet hook size E and medium-weight wool produce an octagon 3in across.
Material and uses Use leftover bulky yarn for a blanket.

This octagon uses 3 colors, A, B and C.
Using A, Make 5ch and join into a ring with a ss into first ch.
Round 1 4ch, 15dc in ring, join with a ss to top of 4ch.
Round 2 5ch, *1dc in back loop only of next st, 2ch; repeat from * to end of round, join with a ss to 3rd st of 5ch. Break off A.
Round 3 Join in B to any dc, 3ch, *2dc in next 2ch space, 1dc in next dc, 4ch, 1dc in next dc; repeat from * 6 more times, 2dc in next 2ch space, 1dc in next dc, 4ch, join with a ss to top of first 3ch. Break off B.
Round 4 Join in C to ss, 1ch, working into back loops only, 1hdc in each st of previous round. Fasten off.

Peach sorbet

Size Crochet hook size E and medium-weight wool produce an octagon 2¾in across.
Materials and uses Make an afghan from acrylic yarn.

This octagon uses 2 colors, A and B.
Using A make 6ch and join into a ring with a ss into first ch.
Round 1 2ch, 23dc in ring, join with a ss to top of 2ch.
Round 2 4ch, 1dc in same st, 1ch, *miss 2 sts, (1dc, 2ch, 1dc) in next st, 1ch; repeat from * 6 more times, join with a ss to 2nd st of 4ch. Break off A.
Round 3 Join in B, 2ch, (1dc, 2ch, 2dc) in first 2ch space, *1dc in 1ch space, (2dc, 2ch, 2dc) in next 2ch space; repeat from * 6 more times, 1dc in last 1ch space, join with a ss to top of 2ch.
Round 4 1sc in each st, 2sc in each 2ch space to end of round, join with a ss to first sc. Fasten off.

Catherine wheel

Size Crochet hook size C and lurex yarn produce a design 4in across.
Materials and uses Make an appliqué motif for a cushion from fine cotton, or use medium-weight cotton for coasters.

Wind yarn 20 times around one finger, then slip loop off finger. Catch ring together with a ss.
Round 1 Work 21sc into ring, join with a ss to first sc.
1st "arm" 10ch, fasten a safety-pin to 10th ch, work 20sc back over 10ch, ss into next sc of round 1, turn, (4ch, miss 4sc, 1sc into next sc) 4 times, turn, (6sc into next 4ch loop) 4 times, miss next sc on round 1, join with a ss to following sc, turn.
2nd "arm" 10ch, ss to center sc of 2nd loop from center, turn, work 20 sc into 10ch loop, ss into next sc of round 1, complete "arm" as before. Work 5 more "arms" and join last to the first with a ss into place marked with a safety-pin, working (3sc, ss, 3sc) into 3rd 4ch loop instead of 6sc, 6sc into 4th 4ch loop, ss into last sc in ring. Fasten off.

Striped octagon

Size Crochet hook size E and medium-weight wool produce an octagon 5¾in across (7 rounds worked).

Materials and uses Make a blanket from leftover knitting worsted or bulky yarn, or use novelty yarn or bouclé for a cushion cover.

This octagon uses 2 colors, A and B. Using A, make 5ch and join into a ring with a ss into first ch.

Round 1 3ch to count as first dc, 15dc into ring, join with a ss to 3rd of first 3ch (16 sts). Break off A.

Round 2 Join in B, 3ch to count as first dc, 2dc at base of 3ch, *1dc into next dc, 3dc into next dc; repeat from * 6 more times, 1dc into next dc, join with a ss to 3rd of first 3ch (32sts). Break off B.

Round 3 Join in A, 3ch to count as first dc, *3dc into next dc, 1dc into each of next 3dc; repeat from * 6 more times, 3dc into next dc, 1dc into each of next 2dc, join with a ss to 3rd of first 3ch (48 sts). Break off A.

Round 4 Join in B, 3ch to count as first dc, 1dc into next dc, *3dc into next dc, 1dc into each of next 5dc; repeat from * 6 more times, 3dc into next dc, 1dc into each of next 3dc, join with a ss to 3rd of first 3ch (64 sts). Break off B.

Continue in this way, increasing 16 sts on each round, working 3dc into dc at each corner, and changing color every round, until octagon is the required size. Fasten off.

Filet octagon

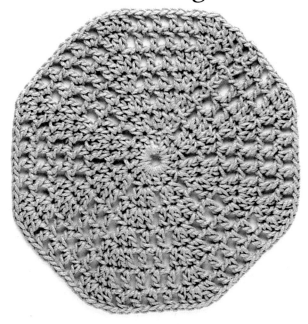

Size Crochet hook size E and crêpe cotton produce an octagon 6in across (7 rounds worked).

Materials and uses Use medium-weight cotton for place mats and coasters, or make a cushion cover from bulky yarn.

Make 6ch and join into a ring with a ss into first ch.

Round 1 3ch, 15dc into ring, join with a ss to 3rd of first 3ch (16sts).

Round 2 3ch to count as first dc, 2dc into base of 3ch, *1ch, miss next dc, 3dc into next dc; repeat from * 6 more times, 1ch, miss next dc, join with a ss to 3rd of first 3ch (8 1-ch spaces).

Round 3 3ch to count as first dc, *3dc into next dc, 1dc into next dc, 1ch, 1dc into next dc; repeat from * 6 more times, 3dc into next dc, 1dc into next dc, 1ch, join with a ss to 3rd of first 3ch.

Round 4 4ch to count as first dc and 1ch space, miss next dc, *3dc into next dc, 1ch, miss next dc, 1dc into next dc, 1ch, 1dc into next dc, 1ch, miss next dc; repeat from * 6 more times, 3dc into next dc, 1ch, miss next dc, 1ch, join with a ss to 3rd of first 4ch (24 1-ch spaces).

Round 5 4ch to count as first dc and 1ch space, 1dc into next dc, *3dc into next dc, (1dc into next dc, 1ch) 3 times, 1dc into next dc; repeat from * 6 more times, 3dc into next dc, (1dc into next dc, 1ch) twice, join with a ss to 3rd of first 3ch.

Round 6 4ch to count as first dc and 1ch space, 1dc into next dc, 1ch, miss next dc, *3dc into next dc, 1ch, miss next dc, (1dc into next dc, 1ch) 4 times, miss next dc; repeat from * 6 more times, 3dc into next dc, 1ch, miss next dc, (1dc into next dc, 1ch) twice, join with a ss to 3rd of first 4ch (40 1-ch spaces).

Continue in this way, increasing 16 1-ch spaces on every alternate round, working 3dc into dc at each corner until octagon is the required size. Fasten off.

Butterfly wings

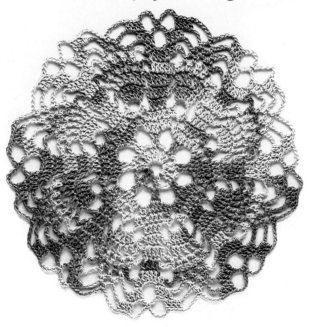

Size Crochet hook size 7 and very fine cotton produce a circle 5in across.

Materials and uses Use very fine cotton for cocktail coasters.

Make 10ch and join into a ring with a ss into first ch.

Round 1 3ch, dc in ring, (3ch, 2dc in ring) 7 times, 3ch, join with a ss to 3rd st of 3ch.

Round 2 3ch, dc in next dc, (5ch, dc in next 2dc) 7 times, 5ch, join.

Round 3 3ch, dc in next dc, *in next space make 3dc, 2ch and 3dc, dc in next 2dc; repeat from * around, join.

Round 4 3ch, dc in next 2dc, *in next space make 2dc, 5ch and 2dc, miss 2dc, dc in next 4dc; repeat from * around, join.

Round 5 3ch, dc in next 2dc, *3ch, 6tr in next space, 3ch, miss 2dc, dc in next 4dc; repeat from * around, join.

Round 6 3ch, dc in next 2dc, *4ch, (dc in next tr, 2ch) 5 times, dc in next tr, 4ch, dc in next 4dc; repeat from * around, join.

Round 7 3ch, dc in next 2dc, *5ch, miss next space, sc in next space, (3ch, sc in next space) 4 times, 5ch,

miss next space, dc in next 4dc; repeat from * around, join.

Round 8 3ch, dc in next 2dc, *6ch, sc in next 3ch loop, (3ch, sc in next loop) 3 times, 6ch, dc in next 4dc; repeat from * around, join.

Round 9 3ch, dc in next 2dc, 2dc in next space, *6ch, sc in next loop, (3ch, sc in next loop) twice, 6ch, 2dc in space, dc in next 4dc, 2dc in next space; repeat from * around, join.

Round 10 Ss in next 3dc, 3ch, dc in next dc, 2dc in next space, *6ch, sc in next loop, 3ch, sc in next loop, 6ch, 2dc in next space, dc in next 2dc, 4ch, miss 4dc, dc in next 2dc, 2dc in next space; rep from * around, join.

Round 11 Ss in next 2dc, 3ch, dc in next dc, 2dc in next space, *6ch, sc in next loop, 6ch, 2dc in next space, dc in next 2dc, 6ch, sc in next space, 6ch, miss 2dc, dc in next 2dc, 2dc in next space; repeat from * around, join. Fasten off.

Spinning wheel

Size Crochet hook size E and medium-weight wool produce a circle 3½in across.

Materials and uses Make a bedspread from medium-weight yarn or knitting worsted, or use fine cotton for a lacy shawl.

Note *Picot (pc): 3ch, 1hdc in top of last hdc.*
Make 6ch and join into a ring with a ss into first ch.
Round 1 5ch (1tr, 2ch in ring) 11 times, join with a ss to 3rd ch.
Round 2 1sc in first 3ch space, 2ch, 2tr, leaving last loop of each tr on hook, yo and draw through 3 loops, 3ch, in each ch space *3tr leaving last loop of each tr on hook, yo and draw through 4 loops − 1 cluster made −, 3ch; repeat from * 10 more times, join with a ss to top of first st.
Round 3 (3hdc, 1pc, 2hdc) in each

space, join with a ss to top of first st. After joining the circles together, the spaces between them may be filled with filler motifs.

Filler motif
Note *Picot (pc): 3ch, 1hdc in top of last sc.*
Make 6ch and join into a ring with a ss into first ch.
Round 1 3ch, 1hdc in ss, *1sc, 1dc, 1tr, 1dtr, 1tr, 1dc, 1sc, 1pc; repeat from * 2 more times, 1sc, 1dc, 1tr, 1dtr, 1tr, 1dc, 1sc, join with a ss to top of first ch. Fasten off.

Scallops and circles

Size Crochet hook size 7 and very fine cotton produce a circle 7¼in across.
Materials and uses Make doilies or place mats from fine cotton.

Make 8ch and join into a ring with a ss into first ch.
Round 1 1ch, 12sc in ring, join with a ss to first sc.
Round 2 4ch, *dc in next sc, 1ch; repeat from * around, joining last 1ch with a ss in 3rd st of starting chain.
Round 3 6ch, dc in same places as ss, *in next dc make dc, 3ch and dc; repeat from * around, join with a ss to 3rd st of starting chain.
Round 4 1ch, make 5sc in each 3-ch space around, join.
Round 5 7ch, *miss next sc, tr in next sc, 3ch; repeat from * around, join with a ss to 4th st of starting chain.
Round 6 4ch, tr in next tr, *5ch, holding back on hook the last loop of each tr make tr in same place as last tr, tr in next tr, yarn over and draw through all loops on hook (a joined tr made); repeat from * around, join.

Round 7 Make 5sc in each 5-ch space around, join.
Round 8 Ss in next 2sc, 9ch, *miss 4sc, tr in next sc, 5ch; repeat from * around, joining last 5-ch with a ss in 4th st of starting chain.
Round 9 As round 6, having 7-ch spaces instead of 5-ch spaces.
Round 10 Make 9sc in each 7-ch space around, join.
Round 11 Ss in next 4sc, 4ch, 2-tr cl in same place as last ss, *5ch, 2-tr cl in 5th ch from hook, miss 8sc, 3-tr cl in next sc; rep from * around, join.
Round 12 4ch, 2-tr cl in same place as ss, *6ch, 2-tr cl in 5th ch from hook, 1ch, 3tr cl in top of next 3-tr cl; rep from * around, join.
Round 13 1ch, sc in same place as ss, *11ch, sc in top of next 3-tr cluster; repeat from * around, join.
Round 14 Work 13sc in each space around, join. Fasten off.

Ruby wine

Size Crochet hook size 7 and very fine cotton produce a circle 5½in across.

Materials and uses Use very fine cotton for coasters, or use any fine yarn for a cushion appliqué motif.

Wind yarn 10 times around one finger, then slip loop off finger.

Round 1 32sc in ring, join with a ss to first sc made.

Round 2 5ch, miss 1sc, dc in next sc, *2ch, miss 1sc, dc in next sc; repeat from * around, ending with 2ch, join with a ss to 3rd st of 5-ch.

Round 3 *10ch, sc in 2nd ch from hook, hdc in next ch, dc in next 7ch, sc in next dc of round 2 (a spoke made); repeat from * around ending with sc at base of 10-ch first made (16 spokes in all).

Round 4 Ss to tip of first spoke, 1ch, sc in tip of same spoke, *7ch, sc in tip of next spoke; repeat from * around, ending with ss in first sc made.

Round 5 5ch, dc in same place as ss, *3ch, sc in next space, 3ch, in next sc make dc, 2ch and dc (shell made); repeat from * around, ending with 3ch, join with a ss to 3rd st of 5-ch.

Round 6 Ss in space, 5ch, dc in same space, *4ch, sc in next sc, 4ch, make a shell in space of next shell; repeat from * around ending with 4ch, join with a ss to 3rd st of 5-ch first made.

Rounds 7–9 As round 6, making shell over shell and sc over sc, having 1 additional st in chs between scs and shells on each successive round. Fasten off.

Prairie rose

Size Crochet hook size C and fine cotton produce a circle 6in across.
Materials and uses Make a bedspread from fine cotton, or use very fine cotton for a motif to be applied to a round cushion.

Make 10ch and join into a ring with a ss into first ch.
Round 1 1ch, (sc in ring, 5ch) 6 times, join with a ss to first sc made (6 spaces).
Round 2 In each loop make sc, hdc, 5dc, hdc and sc (6 petals).
Round 3 *5ch, insert hook in next loop (from back of work) and in following loop (from front of work), yarn over and draw loop through, yarn over and draw through both loops on hook; repeat from * around (6 loops).
Round 4 Work petals as before, making 7 dc (instead of 5) in each petal.
Round 5 Ss in first 3 sts of next petal, sc in next st, *5ch, sc in 3rd ch from hook — picot made —, 3ch, picot, 2ch, miss 3 sts, sc in next st, 2ch, picot, 3ch, picot, 2ch, miss 3 sts of next petal, sc in next st; repeat from * around, join with a ss to first sc made.
Round 6 Ss across to the ch following next picot, ss in loop, 4ch, holding back on hook the last loop of each tr, make 3tr in same loop, yarn over and draw through all loops on hook — cluster made —, 3ch, picot, 5ch, picot, 3ch, make a 4-tr cluster in same loop, in each loop around make cluster, 3ch, picot, 5ch, picot, 3ch and a cluster, join last cluster to top of first cluster. Fasten off.

English rose

Size Crochet hook size D and medium-weight cotton produce an octagon 7¼in across.

Materials and uses Use medium-weight cotton or silky yarn for a bedspread.

Make 10ch and join into a ring with a ss into first ch.

Round 1 1ch, 18sc in ring, join with a ss to first sc made.

Round 2 1ch, sc in same place as ss, *5ch, miss 2sc, sc in next sc; repeat from * 5 more times, 5ch, join with a ss to first sc.

Round 3 1ch, in each loop around make sc, hdc, 5dc, hdc and sc (6 petals), join.

Round 4 1ch, sc in same place as ss, *7ch, insert hook in next loop from back to front of work, bring it out in next loop from front to back of work, yarn over, draw loop through, yarn over and draw through all loops on hook; repeat from * around, join (6 loops).

Round 5 In each loop around make sc, hdc, dc, 7tr, dc, hdc and sc (6 petals).

Round 6 As round 4.

Round 7 Ss in first loop, 3ch, 7dc in same loop, 8dc in each loop around (48dc on round), join with a ss to 3rd st of 3-ch.

Round 8 3ch, dc in next 2dc, *2ch, dc in next 3dc, 4ch, sc in 4th ch from hook − picot made −, dc in next 3dc; repeat from * around, join.

Round 9 3ch, dc in next 2dc, *2ch, dc in next 3dc, 1ch, picot, 1ch, dc in next 3dc; repeat from * around, join.

Round 10 3ch, dc in next 2dc, *2ch, dc in next 3dc, 2ch, picot, 2ch, dc in next 3dc; repeat from * around, join.

Round 11 3ch, dc in next 2dc, *2ch, dc in next 3dc, 11ch, dc in next 3dc; repeat from * around, join.

Round 12 3ch, dc in next 2dc, *2ch, dc in next 3dc, 11dc in next space, dc in next 3dc; repeat from * around, join. Fasten off.

Golden wheel

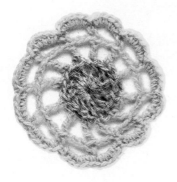

Size Crochet hook size E and medium-weight wool produce a circle 3¼in across.

Materials and uses Use medium-weight or knitting worsted glitter yarn for coasters, or use silky cotton for a bedspread.

This circle uses 2 colors, A and B. Using A, make 5ch and join into a ring with a ss into first ch.

Round 1 5ch, (1tr, 1ch) 11 times in ring, ss in 4th st of 5ch. Break off A.

Round 2 Join in B to any dc, 7ch, miss 1ch, (1tr in back loop only of next st, 3ch, miss 1ch) 11 times, join with a ss to 4th st of 7ch (48sts in round).

Round 3 (4ch, miss 3ch, 1sc in back loop only of next st) 12 times, ending with ss in first st of 4ch.

Round 4 (5hdc in 4ch space, ss in next sc) 12 times. Fasten off.

Satellite

Size Crochet hook size C and fine cotton produce a design 2½in across.

Materials and uses Use fine cotton for tablecloth insertion and border, or use medium-weight cotton for place mats.

Make 5ch and join into a ring with a ss into first ch.

Round 1 1ch, 8sc into ring, join with a ss to first sc made.

Round 2 5ch, *dc in next sc, 2ch; repeat from * until 7 spaces are made, 2ch, ss to 3rd ch of 5-ch, (8 spaces).

Round 3 1ch, sc in joining st, *3sc in 2-ch space, sc in dc; repeat from * around, join with a ss to first sc made.

Round 4 1ch, sc in same space, *7ch, miss 3sc, sc in next st; repeat from * around, join with a ss to first sc (8 loops).

Round 5 *Work 9sc in loop, ss in sc; repeat from * around, join with a ss to last sc. Fasten off.

Floral ring

Size Crochet hook size D and medium-weight cotton produce a circle 5in across.

Materials and uses Make an appliqué motif for a cushion cover from medium-weight cotton or fine multi-colored cotton.

Wind yarn 10 times around one finger, then slip loop off finger. Catch ring together with a ss.
Round 1 4ch, 4tr into ring, (2ch, 5tr into ring) 5 times, 2ch, join with a ss to top of first 4ch.
Round 2 4ch, leaving last loop of each st on hook work 4tr over next 4tr, yo and through all loops on hook − called 4tr cluster −, (6ch, 1dc into next 2ch space, 6ch, leaving last loop of each st on hook work 5tr over next 5tr, yo and through all loops on hook − called 5tr cluster) 5 times, 6ch, 1dc into next 2ch space, 6ch, join with a ss to top of first cluster.

Round 3 Ss to center of next 6ch, 2sc into same loop, *7ch, 2sc into center of next 6ch loop; repeat from * all around, join with a ss to first sc.
Round 4 Ss into next 7ch loop, 3ch, leaving last loop of each st on hook work 3dc into same loop, yo and through all loops on hook − called 3dc cluster −, *9ch, leaving last loop of each st on hook work 4dc into same loop, yo and through all loops on hook − called 4dc cluster −, 4dc cluster into next loop; repeat from * all around, ending with 9ch, 4dc cluster into last loop, join with a ss to top of first cluster. Fasten off.

Sunburst

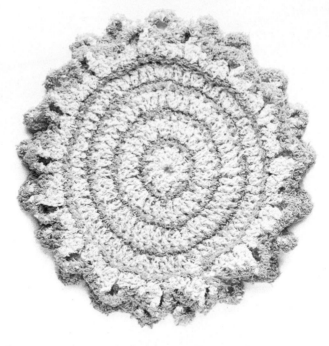

Size Crochet hook size E and cotton bouclé produce a circle 7½in across.

Materials and uses Make coasters from multi-colored cotton, or use thick yarn for plant pot holders.

This circle uses 2 colors, A and B.

Round 1 Using A, 4ch, 11dc in 4th ch from hook, join with a ss to top st of starting chain.

Round 2 Drop A, join in B, 1ch, sc in same place as ss, *2sc in next st, sc in next st; repeat from * around, join with a ss (18sts).

Round 3 Drop B, pick up A, 3ch; 1dc in next st, 2dc in following st to end, join with a ss (32sts).

Round 4 Drop A, pick up B, 1ch; 5sc, 2sc in next st to last 3sts, 3sc, join with a ss (38sts).

Rounds 5 and 6 As rounds 3 and 4, increasing to 52sts and 60sts.

Round 7 As round 3, increasing to 76sts (3dc, 2dc in next st).

Top edging

Round 1 Drop A, pick up B, 1ch, turn and make sc in back loop of each st around, join.

Round 2 Drop B, pick up A, 1ch, sc in same place as ss, *5ch, 3dc where last sc was made, 3sc, sc in next sc; rep from * around, join. Break off A.

Round 3 Pick up B, *5sc in 5-ch loop, sc in next 3dc; repeat from * around. Join and fasten off.

Bottom edging

Join in B and work in remaining free loops of last dc-round of bottom.

Round 1 Sc in each st around, increasing 7sc evenly around (87sts), join.

Round 2 As round 2 of top edging, 2sc instead of 3sts, join and fasten off. Complete as for top edging.

Wheel lace

Size Crochet hook size 7 and very fine cotton produce a circle 2½in across.
Materials and uses Use fine cotton for place mats or a tablecloth, or use medium-weight cotton for a bedspread.

Make 10ch and join into a ring with a ss into first ch.
Round 1 3ch, 23dc in ring, join with a ss to top st of 3-ch.
Round 2 4ch, *dc in next dc, 1ch; repeat from * around, join.
Round 3 Ss in next space, 10ch, *miss 1 space, tr in next space, 6ch; repeat from * around, join last 6-ch with a ss to 4th st of 10-ch.
Round 4 1ch, sc in same place as ss, *2ch, miss 2ch, dc in next ch, 2ch, dc in next ch, 2ch, sc in next tr; repeat from * around, join.
Round 5 1ch, sc in same place as ss, *2ch, dc in next dc, 2ch, dc in 2-ch space, 2ch, dc in next dc, 2ch, sc in next sc; repeat from * around, join. Fasten off.
Subsequent circles may be joined together on the 5th round.
Rounds 1–4 As rounds 1–4 above.
Round 5 1ch, sc in same place as ss, 2ch, dc in next dc, *1ch, ss in corresponding space on first circle, 1ch, dc in next space on 2nd circle, 1ch, ss in next space on first circle, 1ch, dc in next dc on 2nd circle, 2ch, sc in next sc, 2ch, dc in next dc; repeat from * once more, complete round as for first circle.

Ridged octagon

Size Crochet hook size E and medium-weight yarn produce an octagon 3¼in across.

Materials and uses Make a shawl from medium-weight glitter yarn, or use flecked wool or novelty yarn for cushion covers.

Make 5ch and join into a ring with a ss into first ch.

Round 1 5ch, (1dc in ring, 2ch) 7 times, join with a ss to 3rd of 5ch.

Round 2 Ss in 2ch space, 3ch, 4dc in same space, 1ch (5dc in next space, 1ch) 7 times, join with a ss to 3rd ch.

Round 3 3ch *2dc in next dc, yo twice, (bring hook to front of work and inserting hook from right to left, work a tr through bar of next dc) — called tr front, 2dc in next dc, 1dc in next dc, 1ch, 1dc in next dc, rep from * 8 times, omitting 1dc in next dc at end of last rep, join with ss to 3rd ch.

Round 4 1sc in same st as ss (1hdc in next dc, 1dc in next dc, 1tr front in tr front, 1dc in next dc, 1hdc in next dc, 1sc in next dc, 1ss in 1ch space, 1sc in next dc) 8 times, omitting 1sc in next dc at end of last repeat, join with a ss to first sc. Fasten off.
These octagons may be crocheted together on the 4th round.

Rounds 1–3 As rounds 1–3 above.

Round 4 1sc in same st as ss, 1hdc in next dc, 1dc in next dc, 1tr front in tr front, ss to top of a tr front of first octagon, 1dc in next dc on 2nd octagon, 1hdc in next dc, 1sc in next dc, 1ss in 1ch space, 1sc in next dc, 1hdc in next dc, 1dc in next dc, 1tr front in next tr front, ss to top of adjacent tr front of first octagon, complete round as for first octagon. Subsequent octagons may be joined in this way along one, or more sides. The spaces between the octagons may be filled with filler motifs.

Filler motif

Make 5ch and join into a ring with a ss into first ch.

Round 1 3ch, 3dc in ring, ss in space between 2 petals of octagon (4dc in ring of filler motif, ss between 2 petals of adjacent octagon) twice, 4dc in ring of filler motif, ss between 2 petals of remaining octagon, join with a ss to 3rd of 3ch. Fasten off.

FILLERS & MOTIFS

The small motifs in this chapter are particularly useful for filling in spaces left when octagons or circles are joined together. Use the same color and type of yarn, or, for more unusual designs, vary the texture and shade. Alternatively these designs can be used as elements themselves, and joined together. Another way of using them is to incorporate them into a simple net background, or use rows of them as very pretty borders.

Starfish

Size Crochet hook size D and medium-weight cotton produce a motif 3½in across.
Materials and uses Make a matching luncheon set from medium-weight cotton: use single motifs for coasters, join seven together for place mats, use fine cotton for tiny motifs to attach to fabric napkin holders.

Make 5ch and join into a ring with a ss into first ch.
Round 1 2ch, 11hdc in ring, ss in top of 2ch.
Round 2 *7ch, 1hdc in 2nd ch from hook, 1hdc in each of next 4ch, ss in bottom of ch, ss in back loop only of next 2 sts; repeat from * 5 more times.
Round 3 *1sc in each ch of petal, 5sc in turning ch at top of petal, 1 sc in each hdc along other side of petal, ss in st between petals; repeat from * around each petal, ending with ss in st between last and first petal. Fasten off.

Daisy chain

Size Crochet hook size 7 and very fine cotton produce a motif 1½in across.

Materials and uses Make tiny motifs from fine silky or lurex yarn to scatter over an evening shawl, or use cotton crêpe for random appliqué motifs on cushions.

Make 10ch and join into a ring with a ss into first ch.

Round 1 1ch, 18sc in ring, join with a ss to first sc made.

Round 2 4ch (to count as tr), holding back on hook the last loop of each tr make 2tr in same place as ss, yarn over and draw through all loops on hook – 3tr cluster made –, *10ch, miss 2sc, 3tr cluster in next sc; repeat from * around, joining last 10ch with a ss in top of first cluster made.

Round 3 * In next loop make 3sc, (3ch, 3sc) 3 times; repeat from * around. Fasten off.

Cactus flower

Size Crochet hook size C and fine cotton produce a motif 1½in across.

Materials and uses Use pale shades of very fine cotton for scatter appliqué motifs on a christening gown, or use thick cotton yarn and join several together for table mats.

Make 5ch and join into a ring with a ss into first ch.

Round 1 1ch, * sc in ring, 6ch, sc in 2nd ch from hook, hdc in next 4ch, sc in ring, 4ch, sc in 2nd ch from hook, hdc in next 2ch; repeat from * 3 more times, forming 8 petals, ss in first sc made. Fasten off.

To join Sew tips of petals together.

Tumbleweed

Size Crochet hook size B and fine cotton produce a motif 2in across.

Materials and uses Use fine cotton for appliqué motifs around the hem of a little girl's dress, or use as fillers between circles and octagons.

Make 4ch and join into a ring with a ss into first ch.

Round 1 3ch to count as first dc, 11dc into ring, join with a ss to 3rd of first 3ch.

Round 2 * 6ch, ss into 3rd ch from hook to form picot, 4ch, ss into next dc, repeat from * to end, working the last ss into the ss at the end of the first round. Fasten off.

Big wheel

Size Crochet hook size C and fine cotton produce a motif 2½in across.

Materials and uses Make coasters from bulky cotton yarn, or use as a filler motif on larger projects composed of circles or octagons.

Make 7ch and join into a ring with a ss into first ch.
Round 1 3ch, 15dc in ring, join with a ss to top st of 3-ch.
Round 2 7ch, *miss 1dc, dc in next dc, 4ch; repeat from * around, joining last 4-ch with ss in 3rd st of 7-ch (8 spaces).
Round 3 Ss in space, 3ch, 7dc in same space, 8dc in each following space around, join and fasten off.

Green florette

Size Crochet hook size D and medium-weight cotton produce a motif 1½in across.

Materials and uses Decorate cushion covers with motifs made from silky cotton yarn, or use as a filler on larger projects made from circles or octagons.

Make 8ch and join into a ring with a ss into first ch.
Round 1 1ch, 16sc in ring, join with a ss to first sc made.
Round 2 1ch, sc in same place as ss, *5ch, miss 1sc, sc in next sc; repeat from * around, joining last 5-ch to first sc made. Fasten off.

Powder blue

Size Crochet hook size C and fine cotton produce a motif 2½in across.

Materials and uses Use very fine cotton or silk for scatter appliqué motifs on a wedding dress or christening gown, or decorate the edge of a tablecloth or tray cloth with a row of flowers.

Make 8ch and join into a ring with a ss into first ch.

Round 1 3ch, 2dc in ring, (5ch, sc in 3rd ch from hook, 2ch, 3dc, 3dc in ring) 6 times, 5ch, sc in 3rd ch from hook, 2ch, ss in top st of 3-ch.

Round 2 Sc in next dc, (10ch, sc in center dc of next group) 6 times, 10ch, ss in first sc. Fasten off.

Little wheel

Size Crochet hook size 7 and very fine cotton produce a motif 1in across.

Materials and uses Make tiny motifs from fine silky yarn or lurex to scatter around the neckline of an evening blouse, or use medium-weight cotton to decorate place mats and napkin holders.

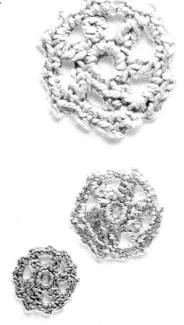

Make 6ch and join into a ring with a ss into first ch.

Round 1 1ch, 12sc in ring, join with a ss to first sc.

Round 2 3ch, dc in same sc used for joining, *3ch, miss next sc, holding back on hook last loop of each dc make 2dc in next sc, yo and draw through all 3 loops on hook – called cluster –; repeat from * 4 more times, 3ch, join with a ss to top of first dc.

Round 3 1ch, (sc, 2ch, sc) in each 3-ch space twice, join with a ss to first sc. Fasten off.

Crème de menthe

Size Crochet hook size C and fine cotton produce a motif 3½in across.
Materials and uses Use medium-weight yarn for random appliqué motifs on cushions, or use fine silky cotton to trim tablecloth or tray-cloth edges.

Make 10ch and join into a ring with a ss into first ch.
Round 1 4ch, 27tr in ring, join with a ss to 4th st of 4-ch.
Round 2 Sc in same place as ss, *5ch, miss 1tr, sc in next tr; repeat from * around, ending with 1ch, tr in first sc made.

Round 3 Ss in loop formed by 1-ch and tr, 4ch, holding back on hook the last loop of each tr make 3tr in same loop, yarn over and draw through all loops on hook – a 3-tr cluster made –, (7ch, 4-tr cluster in next loop) 13 times, 7ch, ss into top of first cluster. Fasten off.

FRUIT & FLOWERS

Realistic three-dimensional designs can be achieved in crochet by using a bobble or embossed technique, or by working twice into the same round, or by joining two or more separate pieces. The fruit and flower patterns in this chapter range from tiny motifs like the Forget-me-not, *p.90, to larger designs such as the* Bunch of grapes, *p.87. These designs can be used to good effect singly, as brooches or to decorate haircombs, hatbands, lapels and pockets; they also look attractive when rows or clusters of them are used.*

Rose Red

Size Crochet hook size B and fine cotton produce a motif 2¼in across.
Materials and uses Decorate a hatband with motifs made from fine cotton, or use silk thread for delicate flowers to trim a neck edge.

Make 8ch and join into a ring with a ss into first ch.
Round 1 6ch, *1dc in ring, 3ch; repeat from * 4 more times, 1ss into 3rd of 6ch.
Round 2 Into each space work 1sc, 1hdc, 3dc, 1hdc and 1sc (6 petals).
Round 3 *5ch, 1sc into next dc of round before last, inserting hook from back; repeat from * ending with 5ch.
Round 4 Into each space work 1sc, 1hdc, 5dc, 1hdc and 1sc.
Round 5 *7ch, 1sc into next sc of round before last, inserting hook from back; repeat from *ending with 7ch.
Round 6 Into each space work 1sc, 1hdc, 7dc, 1hdc and 1sc, 1ss into first sc. Fasten off.

Cherries

Size Crochet hook size B and fine cotton produce cherries 1in across and leaves 1in long.

Materials and uses Use medium-weight yarn for a pocket or lapel appliqué motif or decorate children's clothing with tiny cherries made from fine cotton.

This design uses 4 colors, A, B, C and D.

Background
Using A, make a round medallion as on p.63.

Berries
Using B, make 4ch.
Base row 8tr into 4th ch from hook, turn.
Next row 3ch, *leaving last loop of each tr on hook work 1tr into each of next 5tr − 5 loops on hook −, yo, draw through all loops on hook; repeat from * once more. Fasten off. Make one more berry.

Leaves
Using C, make 8ch.
Next row 1sc into 2nd ch from hook, 1hdc into next ch, 1dc into each of next 3ch, 1hdc into next ch, 3sc into last ch, working down other side of ch, work 1hdc into next ch, 1dc into each of next 3ch, 1hdc into next ch, 1sc into last ch. Fasten off.
Make one more leaf in the same way.
Sew leaves and berries on to background, padding berries with a small amount of spare yarn, and embroider stems with yarn D as illustrated.

Bunch of grapes

Size Crochet hook size F and knitting worsted produce a motif 6in long, 3¼in wide.

Materials and uses Use a single motif made from medium-weight yarn for a pocket appliqué, or use fine cotton to decorate place mats and napkin holders.

This design uses 2 colors, A and B.

Grapes

Using A, make 2ch.

Base row 3sc into 2nd ch from hook.

Next row 1ch, 1sc into first sc, leaving last loop of each st on hook work 5dc into next sc, yo and draw through all loops on hook − called cluster −, 1sc into last sc, turn.

Next row 1ch, 2sc into first sc, 1sc into top of cl, 2sc into next sc, turn.

Next row 1ch, 1sc into first sc, (1 cluster into next sc, 1 sc into next sc) twice, turn (2 clusters).

Next row 1ch, 2sc into first sc, 1sc into each st to last sc, 2sc into last sc, turn (7sc).

Next row 1ch, 1 sc into first sc, *1 cluster into next sc, 1 sc into next sc; repeat from * to end, turn, (3 clusters). Repeat last 2 rows until there are 6 clusters.

Next row 1ch, miss first st, 1sc into

each of next 11sts, turn.

Next row 1ch, 1sc into first st, *1 cluster into next sc, 1 sc into next sc; repeat from * to end (5 clusters). Fasten off.

Leaf

Using B, make 7ch.

Base row 1sc into 2nd ch from hook, 1sc into each of next 5ch, turn.

Next row 1ch, 1sc into each of next 2sc, (1hdc, 1dc) into next sc, (1dc, 1tr, 3ch, 1sc) into next sc, (1hdc, 1dc) into next sc, 3dc into sc at top of leaf, (1dc, 1hdc) into next sc down second side of leaf, (1sc, 3ch, 1tr, 1dc) into next sc, (1dc, 1hdc) into next sc, 1sc into each of last 2sc. Fasten off. Make a second leaf in the same way, ending with 12ch for stalk, 1sc into 2nd ch from hook, 1sc into each ch to end. Fasten off. Sew grapes to leaves and then use as an appliqué motif.

Poppy

Size Crochet hook size D and medium-weight yarn produce a flower 2¾in across.

Materials and uses Embellish the edge of a pot plant holder with poppies made from fine cotton, or use several to decorate place mats and napkin holders.

This flower uses 2 colors, A and B. With A, make 6ch and join into a ring with a ss into first ch.

Round 1 1ch, 7sc into ring, 8sc, join with a ss to first ch.

Round 2 1ch, ★ 2sc into next sc; repeat from ★ to end, join with a ss to first ch (17sc).

Round 3 1ch, 16sc into ring, working into ring over first 2 rounds, join with a ss to first ch. Break off A.

Round 4 (petal) Join in B, 1ch, 1sc into each of next 4sc, turn, ★ 1ch, sc into st at base of ch, 1sc into each sc, 2sc into turning chain, ★, turn; repeat from ★ to ★ once more, (9sc), work 2 rows straight on these sc, turn, 1 sc, work 2sc tog, 1sc into each of next 3sc, 2sc tog, 1sc into turning chain, turn, 1ch, 2sc tog, 1sc into next sc, 2sc tog, 1sc into turning chain, turn, omit 1ch and first sc, 1sc into each of next 2sc, 2sc tog. Fasten off.

Make 3 more petals in same way, beginning each petal in same place as last st of last petal and working last sc of last petal into same place as first on first petal.

Round 5 1ch, 1sc into each st round all petals. Break off B.

Round 6 (stamens) Rejoin A round stem of any sc worked in last center round, ★ 6ch, ss into 2nd ch and each ch to center, sc round stem of next sc; repeat from ★ to end, join with a ss to first ch. Fasten off.

Daffodil

Size Crochet hook size D and medium-weight wool produce a flower 2½in across.

Materials and uses Decorate hair combs or barrettes with flowers made from fine cotton, or use wool or cotton crêpe for lapel or pocket motifs.

This flower uses 3 colors, A, B and C.

Using A, make 4ch and join into a ring with a ss into first ch.

Round 1 2ch to count as first hdc, 5hdc into ring, join with a ss to 2nd of first 2ch (6hdc). Break off A.

Round 2 Join in B, * 7ch, 1sc into 3rd ch from hook, 1sc into each of next 4ch, 1ss into next sc, 1sc into next sc; repeat from * to end, join with a ss to first ch (3 petals), turn.

Round 3 1ch to count as first sc, 1sc into each of next 5sc working into back loop only of each st up side of petal, * (1sc, 1ch, 1sc) into top of petal, 6sc down side of petal, miss ss and next sc, 6sc up side of petal working into back loop only of each st; repeat from * once more, (1sc, 1ch, 1sc), 6sc down side of last petal, miss ss and last sc, join with a ss to first ch. Work into back loop only of each st from now on.

Round 4 1ch to count as first sc, * 1sc into each sc to top of petal, (1sc, 2ch, 1sc) into 1ch sp at top, 1sc into each sc to bottom of petal, miss 2 sts at base; repeat from * 3 more times,

join with a ss to first ch.

Round 5 As round 4. Fasten off. This completes one petal section. Make another in the same way.

Round 6 With ridged side of flower facing and using C work under both loops of each st from now on in normal way, rejoin C to one half dc at center of one petal section, 1ch to count as first sc, 1sc into st at base of ch, 2sc into each hdc all around.

Round 7 * 1ch to count as first sc, 1sc into each sc to end, join with a ss to first ch.

Round 8 1ch to count as first sc, 1sc into st at base of ch, * 1sc into each of next 2sc, 2sc into next sc; repeat from * to last 2 sts, 1sc into each of next 2sts, join with a ss to first ch.

Round 9 As round 7.

Round 10 2ch to count as first sc and picot point, 1ss into 2nd ch from hook, * 1sc into next sc, 1ch, 1ss into top of st just worked; repeat from * to end, join with a ss to first ch. Fasten off.

To finish Sew second petal section to first so that petals lie between petals of first section.

Forget-me-not

Size Crochet hook size D and medium-weight wool produce a flower 1½in across.

Materials and uses Use glitter yarn for random appliqué motifs scattered over an evening shawl, or use fine cotton for a pretty border around a tray cloth.

This flower uses 2 colors, A and B. Using A, make 6ch and join into a ring with a ss into first ch.

Round 1 1ch, 8sc in ring, join with a ss to back loop of first sc. Break off A.

Round 2 Join in B, *3ch, holding back on hook the last loop of each dc make 3dc in same back loop where last ss was made, yarn over and draw through all 4 loops on hook − called cluster −, 3ch, ss in same back loop, ss in back loop of next sc; repeat from * around, ending with ss in same back loop where last cluster was made (8 petals made).

Round 3 Working in front loops of scs on round 1, ss in front loop of first sc, 5ch, ss in 3rd ch from hook − called picot −, * hdc in front loop of next sc, 3ch, complete a picot; repeat from * around (8 picots), join with a ss to 2nd ch of 5-ch at beginning of round. Fasten off.

ANIMALS & OBJECTS

Most of the patterns in this section are given in chart form, read the chart upwards from the bottom right hand corner. These designs are particularly suitable for children's articles, but using squared paper and a little imagination it is easy to design your own patterns. Remember to keep the design simple, without too many color changes.

Gingerbread man

Size Crochet hook size C and knitting worsted produce a motif 4in wide and 4¾in high.

Materials and uses Decorate a child's jumper or overalls with a motif made from machine-washable yarn, or use fine or very fine cotton and sew a string of tiny gingerbread men around the hem or neck of a sweater.

Make 20 ch.
Base row 1dc into 4th ch from hook, 1dc into each ch to end, turn (18dc).
Next row Ss over 6dc, 3ch, miss next dc, 1dc into each of next 5dc, turn.
Next row 3ch, miss first dc, 1dc into each of next 5dc, turn.
Next row (legs) 3ch, miss first dc, 1dc into each of next 2dc, turn, 3ch. Work 3 rows in dc on these 3dc. Fasten off. Rejoin yarn at beginning of legs and work another leg to match.
Head With RS facing, rejoin yarn to 8th dc along 'arms', 3ch, miss first dc, 1dc into each of next 3dc, turn.

Next row 3ch, 1dc into first dc, 2dc into each dc to end, turn.
Next row 3ch, miss first dc, 1dc into each dc to end, turn.
Next row 2ch, 1dc in next dc, *(yo, insert hook into next dc, yo, draw lp through, yo, draw through 2 lps) twice, yo, draw through all lps on hook; rep from * to end, turn. Work 1 row of sc all around gingerbread man. Fasten off.
To finish Using leftover black yarn, embroider eyes, mouth and buttons as illustrated.

Duck

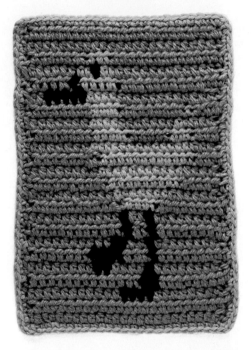

Size Crochet hook size D and knitting worsted produce a rectangle 5½in by 7½in.

Materials and uses Use bulky yarn or knitting worsted for a blanket, or make pockets for overalls from machine-washable yarns.

This design uses 3 colors, A, B and C.

Note *To change color, before drawing through last 2 loops of last dc of one color group, drop this color, pick up the other color, yarn over and draw through the 2 loops on hook. Continue with other color, carrying the dropped color along top of previous row and working over it to conceal it.*

Using A, make 27ch.

Row 1 Dc in 4th ch from hook and in each ch across (25dc, counting turning ch as 1dc), 3ch, turn.

Row 2 Dc in each dc, dc in top st of turning ch.

Row 3 Holding yarn B along top of previous row, with A dc in 9dc (thus concealing B), changing yarn in last dc. With yarn B dc in 4dc, carrying yarn A concealed in dcs and changing yarn at last dc. With yarn A dc in

12dc, 3ch, turn.

Rows 4–25 Continue following chart, carrying unused yarn and changing yarn as in row 3.

To finish Using C, work one row of single crochet all around the edge.

Each square represents 1dc

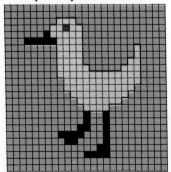

Row 1

92

Teddy bear

Size Crochet hook size D and medium-weight yarn produce a square 6in across.

Materials and uses Make a carriage cover using wool crêpe or medium-weight yarn, or sew four or more squares together for cushions for a child's room.

This design uses 3 colors, A, B and C.

Note *To change color, before drawing through last 2 loops of last dc of one color group, drop this color, pick up the other color, yarn over and draw through the 2 loops on hook. Continue with other color, carrying the dropped color along top of previous row and working over it to conceal it.*

Using A, make 42ch.

Row 1 Dc in 4ch from hook and in each ch across (40dc, counting turning chain as 1dc), 3ch, turn.

Rows 2 and 3 Dc in each dc, dc in top st of turning chain, 3ch, turn.

Row 4 Holding yarn B along top of previous row, with yarn A dc in 3dc (thus concealing yarn B), changing color in the last dc. With yarn B dc in 6dc, carrying yarn A concealed in dcs and changing color in the last dc. With yarn A dc in 20dc, carrying yarn B concealed in dcs and changing color in last dc. With yarn B dc in 6dc, carrying yarn A concealed in dcs

and changing colors in last dc. With yarn A dc in 4dc, 3ch, turn.

Rows 5–20 Continue following chart, introducing yarn C and carrying unused yarn and changing yarn as in row 4.

To finish Work a row of single crochet edging all around, and embroider eyes, nose and mouth as illustrated.

Each square represents 2dc

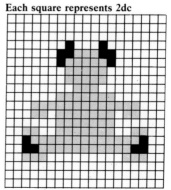

Row 1

Butterfly

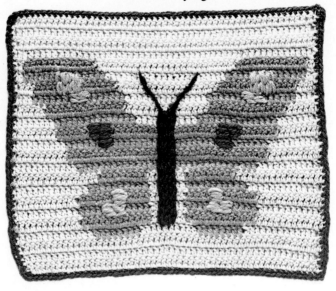

Size Crochet hook size D and medium-weight yarn produce a rectangle 8in by 6in.

Materials and uses Make an afghan from bulky yarn, alternating butterfly squares with plain squares, or use thick cotton yarn for place mats, working each mat in different shades.

This design uses 4 colors, A, B, C and D.

Note *To change color, before drawing through last 2 loops of last dc of one color group, drop this color, pick up the other color, yarn over and draw through the 2 loops on hook. Continue with other color, carrying the dropped color along top of previous row and working over it to conceal it.*

Using A, make 56ch.

Row 1 Dc in 4th ch from hook and in each ch across (54dc, counting turning ch as 1dc), 3ch, turn.

Row 2 Dc in each dc, dc in top st of turning ch.

Row 3 As row 2.

Row 4 Holding yarn B along top of previous row, with A dc in 14dc (thus concealing B), changing yarn in last dc. With B dc in 8dc, carrying A concealed in dcs and changing yarn in last dc. With A dc in 10dc, carrying B concealed in dcs and changing yarn in the last dc. With yarn B dc in 8dc, carrying A concealed in dcs and changing yarns in last dc. With A dc in 14dc, 3ch, turn.

Rows 5–23 Continue following chart, carrying unused yarn and changing yarn as in row 4.

To finish Using C and D embroider body, antennae, and pattern on wings. Work one row of single crochet all around the edge.

Each square represents 2dc

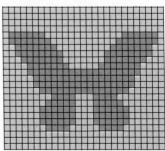

Row 1

Index

Acknowledgements

Samples
June Briggs

Artist
John Hutchinson

Photographer
Ian O'Leary

Typesetting
Cambrian Typesetters

Reproduction
Newsele SRL